HOSHIN GAMES

By

Shihan John Porter, Ph.D., M. Ed.

Other Books offered by Hoshin Budo Ryu (HBR)

Hoshin Healing Manual
Mandala Therapy
The Psions' Guide
The Unabridged Dictionary of Mysticism, Spiritualism, and the Supernatural
Compilation of Hoshin E-mails (The best questions and answers from members since 1997 to present)
Hoshin Dim Mak (Fire belts and up)

Hoshin Games

Published by
Hoshin Budo Ryu
www.hoshin.us

Original cover design by Dr. John Porter
Typeset & Pictures by Jared Guinn

ISBN 978-0-6151-8525-5

John Porter has studied martial arts his entire life, over the past three decades focusing *on Ninpo Ninjutsu (4th dan)* and *Hoshin (6th dan)*. Dr. Porter has mastered the use of psi skills and has used them extensively to achieve success in his life's pursuits. Dr. Porter has a *Bachelor's degree in Eastern Philosophy*, a *Masters in Physical Education*, a *Masters in Special Education*, and *a Doctorate in Behavioral Psychology*. Through the implementation of the concepts of *Mandala Therapy* and *Psionics*, Dr. Porter has achieved *State Championships in Basketball and Track and Field*, both as a player and as a coach, qualified for the 1980 U.S. Olympic Trials in the Decathlon with a world class score of 7658, and participated in *Cross-Country Horseback Riding* and the *Modern Pentathlon*. He is a licensed *Sailing Captain*. He has been named in the *Who's Who in Business, Who's Who in Martial Arts*, and as an *Outstanding Young American*, and served on the *Ohio Small Business Development Council.*

PREFACE

'The MOOK and the Tennis Balls'

Each year we sponsor at least one urban adventure activity. One year we were doing a version of an espionage activity. Participants have a degree of autonomy within these activities. There are several sky walks in downtown Cincinnati connecting many of the buildings. This particular activity took place on the sky walks and the connecting buildings. Tennis balls were used as weapons. If you got hit, you had to give up your weapon, or information that you had gathered during the activity. To start the activity, the group gathered at the bottom of one of the stairs leading up to the sky walk.

There are several methods we use to choose the order of participants. This day we chose to start in chronological order. Participants started the activity by going up the stairs at two minute intervals. The first player this day was a student known as "The Mook". Two minutes after he went up the stairs the second person went up. As soon as the second person got to the top of the stairs, *whaapp!* He was hit by the Mook's tennis ball. After returning down the stairs to restart, the next participant went up the stairs. As soon as the third person got to the top of the stairs, *whaapp!* The Mook held his ground. Two up and two down. It was the fourth person's turn. By this time we were all on guard of an impending ambush at the top of the stairs. He very carefully inched to the top of the stairs. He peeked over the edge of the stair rail in the direction of the previous ambushes. Not seeing anyone, he went up a little further. Then *whaapp!* He was hit in his back. The Mook had gone around behind his original successful sniper position. By the time the fifth person nervously went up, the Mook had moved on down the skywalk to find other sniper positions. This was one of the most memorable experiences in our urban survival classes.

Jeff and the 'Beating of a Tree'

One of my favorite activities is playing capture the flag in the woods. These activities often provided the opportunity to practice map reading skills, communication skills, stealth, traps, PSI, and so on. Trees in particular have been found to be very effective in projecting energy upon.

On one particular night activity, Jeff, stealthily made his way down the side of an embankment to position himself in an attacking position. All of a sudden he rose up and ran to attack the person he had targeted. He began to beat away, flailing with weapons in both hands against the target person. After about thirty seconds of fighting he stopped hitting because the target person wasn't fighting back, nor moving. Even Jeff thought this to be strange. It was a few seconds later that he realized he had been attacking a tree, rather than a person. The Psion, now standing beside him, had projected his energy into the tree.

TABLE OF CONTENTS

PSIONICS

PROBLEM SOLVING

PHYSICAL TECHNIQUES

Objective: Describes the expected outcome of the activity.

Type: Describes which category the activity is under. They are... Warm-up, Urban Playground, Trust, Stealth, Team Building, Survival, Psionics, Problem Solving, and Physical Techniques.

Participants: Either individual, partner, trio, or group.

Individual: Meaning that only one person is needed, therefore, this activity can be conduct at any time the individual wants to work on a particular skill. Although, most of the individual activities can be conducted with a group.

Partner: Activities that require two people to interact in some way to accomplish the goal. There can be several groups of two all doing the activity at the same time.

Trio: Activities that require groups of three people to interact in some way to accomplish the goal. There can be several groups of three all doing the activity at the same time.

Group: Activities that require at least seven people to interact in some way to accomplish the goal. Most of the group activities will accommodate groups of ten to twenty participants. For extremely large groups, it may be more beneficial to divide participants into smaller, more manageable groups.

Materials: Lists the materials needed as well as the location that best suits the activity.

Method: Describes how the game or activity is performed.

Variation: Includes an alternate (often more difficult) method for the activity.

Notes/Clues: Points to look out for when conducting the activity and tips on how to make the whole process function more smoothly.

Learning Styles: Each activity has its' own set of primary learning styles. They are... Deductive, Inductive, Global, Intuitive, Kinesthetic, Multi-sensory, Sequential, Social, Reflective, Rhythmic, Verbal, Visual, and Youthful.

Safety Considerations

Some of the activities, like the warm-up activities, are relative safe in their structure. Other activities may need special safety instructions and precautions.

One of the best ways to become proficient at feeling the technique is to perform it blind folded. While blind folded:

A. Do not run.
B. Do not lead with your head.
C. If you get dizzy, hurt, or lost, take the blind fold off.

WARM-UPS and CONDITIONING

The purpose of these warm-up activities is to get the body, mind, and spirit in the best condition to pursue the training of intermediate and advanced techniques.

HOSHIN GAMES

ARM HANG

Objective: To develop arm and hand strength for climbing and stealth.

Type: Warm-up

Participants: Individual

Materials: A bar from one to two inches in diameter, horizontal seven or more feet above the ground.

Method: Jump or step up to the bar. Grab with both hands and hang until you let go. The level required to begin to be in stealth condition is three minutes with controlled breathing.

Variation: Try one-handed hang or using only 2 or 3 fingers.

Learning Style: Kinesthetic, Global

BACK-TO-BACK SIT AND STAND

Objective: To develop balance, coordination, and cooperation.

Type: Warm-up

Participants: Partner

Materials: None

Method: This is a partner activity. Participants will stand back-to-back with their partner. Participants may or may not lock arms, be tied together, or be on uneven surfaces. Participants will move from a standing position to a sitting position and then back to a standing position.

Variation: Individually, put your back to the wall or a tree, and move into a sitting position. Use this posture to rest and relax.

Learning Style: Kinesthetic, Multi-sensory, Social

BALANCE BEAM TRANSFER

Objective: To cooperatively work together while maintaining balance.

Type: Warm-up

Participants: Group

Materials: Long balance beam. Edges of a sand box.

Method: Divide participants into two groups. Each group starts at the opposite end of the balance beam from the other. Each group is to get all of their members to the opposite side. When using a square or rectangular shape, such as a sand box, each group must move in the opposite direction as the other and return to where they started.

Learning Style: Kinesthetic, Intuitive, Sequential

BEAN BAG TOSS (Name Game)

Objective: To learn to help others in a cooperative process.

Type: Warm-up

Participants: Group

Materials: One bean bag for the group.

Method: Participants will stand in a circle. The leader tosses a bean bag to one student, calling that student's name before throwing the bean bag. All throws will be under hand, soft, and so the participant can make an easy catch. The throws should not be to the students standing next to the thrower. When the next participant catches the bean bag they will look to another participant, call that participants name, and toss the bean bag to them. This process will continue until each participant has tossed and caught the bean bag one time, and one time only, and the bean bag is returned to the leader or initial thrower. If not everyone has handled the bean bag once and only once the group must try it again until they are successful.

Variation: To be successful each person must throw to the same person each time. To cause problems for the group, the leader can vary the person they start with.

Learning Style: Kinesthetic, Multi-sensory, Social

BLADE OF GRASS

Objective: To relax and trust others while in an uncontrolled situation.

Type: Warm-up

Participants: Group

Materials: None.

Method: Participants stand in a circle close together. The number of participants forming the circle should be between four and eight. Have another participant stand in the middle of the circle, cross their arms over their chest, close their eyes, relax, and begin to lean. As the center person leans they are caught by circle members and pushed around like a blade of grass in the wind. The person in the center should relax and trust as much as possible.

Learning Style: Kinesthetic, Reflective, Inductive

BLIND SHOE/WEAPONS

Objective: To develop the intuited tactual senses in the hands.

Type: Warm-ups

Participants: Group

Materials: Similar objects of all participants, such as shoes, training weapons, and so forth.

Method: Have each of the participants place their object, similar to the other participants (like a pair of shoes), in a pile across the room. Participants will return to the other side of the room. Participants will then place a blindfold over their eyes. Participants will then walk to the pile of items and correctly select the item that is their own.

Learning Style: Intuitive, Inductive, Multi-sensory

ELBOW TAG

Objective: Develop combined physical and mental reactions under chaos and stress.

Type: Warm-up

Participants: Group

Materials: An outside activity needing lots of space.

Method: Have each person pick a partner, link elbows and form a large circle with sufficient space between partners. One set of partners will be in the middle. Of these two participants, one will be the 'it' (chaser) person and chase the other. The chaser tries to tag the other person before that person can link elbows with another participant. When the person being chased links elbows, the person who is attached to the other elbow of that person must run and hookup with a new elbow of person in another pair before he or she is tagged. When a person is tagged, not joining elbows, he or she becomes the chaser.

Learning Style: Kinesthetic, Intuitive, Inductive.

GEOMETRY

Objective: Giving and following directions.

Type: Warm-up

Participants: Group

Materials: A long rope (100') and blind folds for each participant.

Method: Tie the ends of the rope together making a large loop. Participants are to blind fold themselves and pick up the rope, holding a part of the rope with both hands. A designated group member will verbally instruct members to move so as to form various geometric shapes.

For example, the first shape might be a square. The leader would ask four people, one at a time, to move to form the corners, and then instruct the others to move to form straight lines. Shapes with few corners and straight lines are easiest and should be used as warm-ups and to understand the activity. Shapes with multi-corners and/or circular are more difficult.

Learning Style: Deductive, Kinesthetic, Reflective

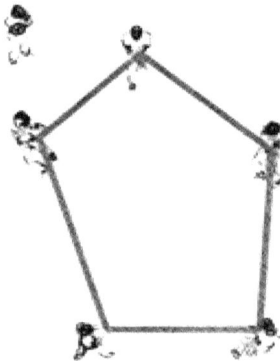

GIANTS, ELVES AND WIZARDS

Objective: To make quick decisions as to attack or defend.

Type: Warm-up

Participants: Group

Materials: This is an outside activity and needs lots of space.

Method: This activity is similar to 'rock, scissors, and paper'. The class is divided into two groups. Each group gets into a huddle to determine if they are going to be Giants, Elves, or Wizards. All students in the group will be the same character for each round. Both teams will line across, parallel from each other in a straight line. Participants will say "one, two, three, and their character". Giants chase Elves, Elves chase Wizards, Wizards chase Giants. If both groups have selected the same character no one chases anyone. The team that is chasing has about five seconds (twenty yards to a safe zone) to tag someone on the other team. When a participant has been tagged they come back to that team. Repeat the process until only one team member remains.

Learning Style: Kinesthetic, Intuitive, Multi-sensory

HOW DO YOU LIKE YOUR TRAINING PARTNER?

Objective: Awareness of self and others. Develop the ability to determine if and when an action needs to be taken.

Type: Warm-up

Participants: Group

Materials: Enough chairs for all participants except one to sit in.

Method: Everyone is seated in a circle with the 'IT' person standing in the middle. 'IT' will go up to anyone who is seated and ask them "How do you like your training partner?" The one who is asked will say, I like all of my training partners, but I especially like the ones wearing; then they would say some descriptor like; white shoes, blue shirt, or sun glasses. As soon as the descriptor word is mentioned, everyone wearing that item, or with that descriptor moves to a new seat. The person who does not get the seat is the new 'IT'. To vary the activity, use personal characteristics, skills, and so forth as the identifying concept.

Learning Style: Visual, Reflective, Intuitive

INSTANT REPLAY

Objective: To learn participants names.

Type: Warm-up

Participants: Group

Materials: None.

Method: Have the participants stand in the circle. Each person will say their name and then make a motion or action that corresponds with their name. The other participants then repeat the person's name and motion. Repeat this process for all students. Have students repeat all students' names and motions as they are said.

Learning Style: Youthful, Sequential, Reflective

John!!!

Sarah!!!

Eric!!!

KNOTS

Objective: Problem solving in close proximity.

Type: Warm-up

Participants: Group

Materials: None.

Method: Divide participants into groups of six to ten people. Each group will stand in a circle facing the other participants. Each person in the circle will reach across and grab the hand of another person in the circle, preferably one not standing directly next to them. Once each person is connected with one hand, then grab the hand of a different participant. Do not grab onto both hands of the same person. The group will then try to untangle itself, into a straight line, without letting go of each other's hand.

Learning Style: Multi-sensory, Kinesthetic, Social

LEG STAND

Objective: To improve balance and focus.

Type: Warm-up

Participants: Individual

Materials: Various surfaces.

Method: Stand on one leg for a period of time. Add activities while standing (i.e. take off an article of clothing and put it back on, juggle, eat and drink, etc.).

Variation: Perform this exercise on your tip-toes and try the same activities. Notice the differences in the difficulty.

Learning Style: Multi-sensory, Inductive, Reflective

LIFT (GROUP TRUST)

Objective: To build group confidence and cohesion.

Type: Warm-up

Participants: Group

Materials: None.

Method: Have one participant lie prone on the ground, face up, hands across their chest. The other group members will lift the individual over their heads and safely return them to the ground. Start with the smallest participant and proceed to the heaviest group member. The leader should count "one, two, three, lift" and "one, two, three, return." It is very important not to feel overly confident that you have lifted someone, then relax and have them fall to the ground.

Learning Style: Social, Reflective, Intuitive

NAME GAME I

Objective: To learn the names of participants in a large group.

Type: Warm-up.

Participants: Group.

Materials: None.

Method: Participants will stand in a circle. The first participant tells their name. The next participant gives their name, and reintroduces the first participant. Continue this process around the circle, each person introducing themselves and all those that came before them, repeating all names, until everyone is named. For example, the fifth person might say "My name is Eve, this is Darrin, this is Chris, this is Bob, and this is Adam.

Variations: a. Reverse the order of introductions.
b. Randomly introduce everyone.

Learning Style: Youthful, Sequential, Reflective

NAME GAME II

Objective: To learn the names of participants in a large group.

Type: Warm-up

Participants: Group

Materials: None

Method: Participants will go around the circle saying their first name and an animal they like. After the first person, the second person says, "That is Tom, he likes guerrillas; I am (name) and I like (animal)". Each person begins with the first person and says the name and animal of all persons before him or her.

Variation: Tell the participants that they have to pick an animal that starts with the same letter as is in their name. The same animal cannot be named twice.

Learning Style: Youthful, Sequential, Reflective

PARTNER PUSH-UPS

Objective: To develop physical and mental strength, along with confidence and determination.

Type: Warm-up

Participants: Partner

Materials: Various surfaces.

Method: Have both participants in a push-up position. One of the participants has their feet or shins on the other participant's upper back (do not place feet on lower back). Both partners can perform a set of push-ups or just the person on the bottom can do their set. Switch positions after one set.

Warning: Any exercise performed with an extra amount of weight is very hard on the body. Do not over do these types of exercises for they may result in injury. Communicate with your partner if he or she is becoming too heavy.

Learning Style: Kinesthetic, Multi-sensory, Global

PUSH-UPS

Objective: To develop hand speed and confidence.

Type: Warm-up

Participants: Individual

Materials: Various surfaces.

Method:
    a. On knuckles.
    b. Palm down to hand clap.
    c. Knuckles down to hand clap.
    d. Palms down to chest touch.
    e. Knuckles down to chest touch.
    f. Diamond push-ups to clap.
    g. Wide push-ups to clap.
    h. Get 2 or 3 claps.
    i. Palm down to clap behind back.
    j. Knuckles down to clap behind back.
    k. Use only your fingers and thumb.
    l. Take a finger away until only your index and thumbs remain.
    m. Use different surfaces.
    n. Elevate your feet.

Learning Style: Kinesthetic, Multi-sensory, Global

PUSH-OVER

Objective: To listen to and follow directions.

Type: Warm-up

Participants: Partner

Materials: None.

Method: Participants will divide into groups. Standing facing each other with elbows bent and the palm of one person's hands almost touching the palms of the other person. Make sure everyone is in the proper position and ready to go. Explain that you will give them the directions and then you want them to respond as quickly as possible. Then tell the group that "The objective of this activity is to not get pushed back. One, two, three, go!"

Typically, about half the group will begin to push the person across from them. As soon as you see this occur, stop the activity. Explain that some of the group is successful, some are not. Try again. Repeat the directions. To be successful you do not need to push the other person at all. Those who are pushing are too aggressive.

Learning Style: Verbal, Reflective, Multi-sensory

ROPE CIRCLE

Objective: To build team spirit and balance.

Type: Warm-up

Participants: Group

Materials: One large rope, approximately three to four feet for each person participating (A martial arts belt will do).

Method: Participants will stand in a circle. Participants will stand relatively close to each other, probably not more than two or three feet apart. The rope will be tied at the ends to create a large circle. Participants will hold onto the rope with both hands. Participants will then all sit down at the same time, holding onto the rope for balance. The participants will then return to the standing position, using the rope as balance.

Learning Style: Kinesthetic, Multi-sensory, Inductive

WALK A STRAIGHT LINE I

Objective: To learn to move quickly in a dark and/or treacherous environment.

Type: Warm-up

Participants: Individual

Materials: An open field.

Method: Participants are blind folded. They are to walk in a straight line while blind folded. The best location to start is a large field, like a soccer field. Start with a 10 yard to 20 yard distance. Then steadily increase the distance to about a 100 yards.

Variation: Have participants race for a given distance.

Learning Style: Multi-sensory, Intuitive, Kinesthetic

WALK A STRAIGHT LINE II

Objective: To learn to move quickly in a dark and/or treacherous environment.

Type: Warm-up

Participants: Individual, Group

Materials: A wooded forest with little undergrowth is the best place to start.

Method: This is exactly like WALK A STRAIGHT LINE I, except it is carried out in a wooded area. Participants will negotiate trees, shrubs, sloping ground, and other possible obstacles while covering a specific distance.

Variation: If in a group, have one person walk a few yards away from the blindfolded participants. Have that one person hit a tree with a stick or make an audible signal for the blindfolded to follow. First one to find the person making the noise wins. Increase the distance of the noisemaker and the blindfolded for more of a challenge.

Learning Style: Multi-sensory, Deductive, Kinesthetic

YURT CIRCLE

Objective: To practice balance and develop group dynamics.

Type: Warm-up

Participants: Group

Materials: An even number of participants. The leader of the group may or may not be part of the activity, ensuring that there will be an even number in the participating group.

Method: Participants will stand in a circle approximately arm lengths apart. Each participant will face in the opposite direction than the participant standing next to them, relative to facing in or out of the surface. After the entire group is facing the correct way, have the next person in the circle choose a different direction to face. See how fast the whole group can make the switch and continue until each person picks a direction.

Variation:
>   a. Have the participants stand only on their right or left leg as they face their respective directions.
>   b. Have them mimic a certain hand or arm posture from their neighbor.
>   c. Set a very short time limit (3 to 6 seconds)
>   d. Add in a penalty, such as push-ups or sit-ups, if anyone in the group faces the wrong way.

Learning Style: Kinesthetic, Social, Inductive

HOSHIN GAMES

PLAY GROUND

HOSHIN GAMES

CHUTES AND LADDERS

Objective: To practice alternative methods of climbing trees and walls.

Type: Urban Playground

Participants: Individual

Materials: Trees next to buildings or next to each other, within about two to three feet.

Method: The participant will wedge themselves between the tree and wall. Variations of a sitting position or a 'cat back' are the two most common postures for this activity. The participant will climb to the roof of the building (or to the sturdy branches of a tree). This is an easier method of climbing a tree rather than chinning up the tree.

Learning Style: Kinesthetic, Multi-sensory, Inductive

ROOF-TO-ROOF

Objective: To practice urban movement without being seen.

Type: Urban Playground

Participants: Individual

Materials: The roof tops of several connecting or nearly connecting buildings.

Method: The participant will access a roof top in a multi-building business area. The participant will move across the roof tops in an efficient manner and descend to the street level at a second point of entry.

Learning Style: Kinesthetic, Multi-sensory, Inductive

SEESAW WALK

Objective: To improve balance and coordination

Type: Play Ground

Participants: Individual

Materials: A seesaw.

Method: Stand in the middle of a seesaw (teeter-totter) to gain a sense of balance. Then walk from one end of the seesaw to the other, gently allowing the board to raise and lower. Use stealth in quietly touching the ends of the seesaw to the ground.

Learning Style: Kinesthetic, Multi-sensory, Reflective

SLIDE CLIMB

Objective: Develop arm strength for climbing.

Type: Play Ground

Participants: Individual

Materials: A slide at least ten feet high. The higher the slide the better.

Method: There are three climbing angles.

1.) Grab the back of the steps and climb up from under the steps with the arms only. This exercise can also be done with any ladder.

2.) Grab each of the brace poles under the seat, one with each hand. Pull with arms and move hands up until you reach the top. Have a controlled climb back down. Focus on breathing.

3.) Stand under the slide itself. Reach over either side of the slide and grab the rail, one side with each hand. Wrap your legs around the slides of the slide as well. Using the hands and arms only, pull yourself up to the top. Then return in a controlled reverse climb.

Learning Style: Kinesthetic, Multi-sensory, Reflective

SMALL OPENINGS

Objective: To practice escape, fleeing, and pursuit skills.

Type: Urban Playground

Participants: Individual

Materials: Anything that has an opening about the size of the participants' body size, or a little smaller. An example might be a gate that is chained shut, yet has a small gap between the braces or the space between two overlapping pine trees.

Method: The participant will practice going through these areas, testing and measuring the size of an area they can or cannot go through. It is important to find and know where some of these locations are, especially in neighborhoods that are dangerous. If chased, the individual can run to one of these locations and quickly squeeze through, gaining valuable time over their pursuers, or even ending the pursuit itself. Running through the branches of a pine tree will stop most people the first time they attempt it. (Note: Some pine trees have softer needles than others).

Learning Style: Kinesthetic, Intuitive, Global

STAIRS

Objective: To practice evasion and escape skills.

Type: Physical Skill

Participants: Individual

Materials: Use a variety of stairs e.g. long, with landing ways, etc.

Method: This activity is to experiment with ways of going up and down stairs as fast as you can. There are two basic techniques. On stairs with a hand rail, lean down and grab the railing several feet from where you are standing. Use your arms as a lever and vault down several steps at a time. The more this activity is practiced, the more stairs can be covered in a single vault. The second method for going down stairs quickly is to step on each stair in quick, rhythmic pattern. The participant should be able to go down the stairs rapidly without touching the railings or any other object for balance.

Note: Speed movement must include balance and control. An example of an unsuccessful technique on the stairs is when participant makes a long jump and on the landing loses balance and falls. The recovery time to continue will probably be longer than good technique. It also takes the participant out of good posture.

Learning Style: Rhythmic, Kinesthetic, Deductive

SWING WALK

Objective: To develop balance and coordination.

Type: Play Ground

Participants: Individual

Materials: A swing set with multiple swings capable of holding heavy weight.

Method: Using a multi-seat swing set, the more seats the better, start by standing on an end swing seat. Then move the swing seat so that you can step onto the second swing without touching the ground. Continue going from seat to seat, without touching the ground, from one end of the swing set to the other.

Learning Style: Kinesthetic, Intuitive, Sequential.

TRUST ACTIVITIES

Trust activities can be used to bring a group together. If you plan to incorporate small unit strategies and techniques with a consistent group of practitioners you may want to start the training with some group trust activities to build early cohesion. There are some other **TRUST ACTIVITIES** listed and identified in the warm-up section.

HOSHIN GAMES

TRUST FALL

Objective: Develop trust and confidence with your team.

Type: Trust

Participants: Group

Materials: A platform approximately three feet above the ground. At least six participants.

Method: One of the participants will be identified as the person who will be falling backward from a platform. The platform should be about four feet high, or a little higher. Five feet is too definitely too high in most cases. The participant designated to fall will climb up to the platform while the others spot their climb. The remaining participants will then form two lines facing each other with the leader at the head. There should be one person in the catching line for every thirty pounds of the faller. For example, the minimum number to catch a 150 pound person should be five. The minimum number to catch a 210 pound person should be seven. The participant falling will turn their back to the group, fold their arms across their chest, and hold tight. The remainder of the group (at least five) will form a close line by alternating their forearms at ninety degrees with the person across from them to form a catching surface. One person should be designated to catch the head. This person is the leader of the falling activity. This person will also be the person to determine that the conditions are right for the fall and the catch. When everything is ready, and safety is insured, the person on the platform may relax and begin to fall back. The faller should not flail their arms. This presents the most possibility of injury. Once caught, the person at the head will signal to put the falling person on the ground, feet first.

Safety: This is among the most dangerous TRUST ACTIVITIES, although is generally very safe when safety precautions are taken. The leader of the activity should observe the catching surface, making sure that there are no holes. The heaviest part of most people is between their hips and shoulders. Therefore, on bigger people, stronger catchers may be placed in these areas. It is also recommended that a falling command procedure is followed by the faller to make sure everyone is ready to catch them.

Example commands: Faller says, "Ready to fall."
Leader says, "Fall on."

Learning Style: Intuitive, Inductive, Global

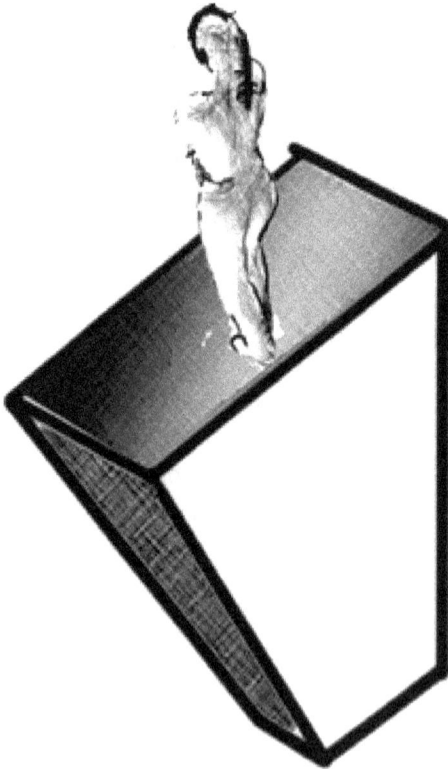

TRUST TAG

Objective: To distinguish and listen to a specific voice, in a group of loud voices during a stressful situation; to trust in following directions under pressure.

Type: Trust

Participants: Group

Materials: One blindfold per group of two.

Methodology: Participants will organize into groups of two. One person in each group will put on a blindfold. Each blindfolded person will have a sighted partner. One group is the "IT" group, whose purpose is to tag the other players. The blindfolded player is the tagger. Sighted partners only give directions to the "it" person. The sighted person gives verbal directions and does not move. Play tag as normal, the person who is "it" tries to tag the other blindfolded players. The partner of each blindfolded player gives direction to how to get to the other person, or how to escape. The sighted person must remain stationary. When a player has been tagged they are also "it" and can tag the remaining players until all players have been tagged.

Learning Style: Verbal, Deductive, Kinesthetic

TRUST WALK

Objective: To develop trust in a team; to negotiate obstacles by a sense of feel.

Type: Trust

Participants: Group

Materials: A community park, woods, etc.

Method: All participants are blindfolded except the leader. All participants hold hands to the person in front of them and to the person behind them. The leader will lead the group on a walk. Start out easy. Walk down a lane, a trail, and take a couple of turns. Once the participants understand the activity and are comfortable with being blindfolded, increase the level of difficulty. Begin to negotiate stairs, walls, benches, and other obstacles. Take the group under low hanging objects. Walk through bushes, water, and narrow places.

Repeat the activity several times. It doesn't matter if you repeat the same day, or over several months. However, have the participants change their line positions from front, middle, back, and leader. Discuss what was experienced and how difficulties and obstacles were handled.

Variations: For more experienced groups communication may be limited, or participants may carry back packs.

Learning Style: Multi-sensory, Social, Global

HOSHIN GAMES

Stealth tactics do not only include the ability of moving and hiding quietly, they also include the ability to control breathing and intention. To truly develop stealth-ness one must become proficient in each of these three areas.

The best place to start with stealth skills is to practice basic stealth walking. The following is a list of basic stealth walking techniques.

I. Moving and Hiding Quietly

1. Walking: basic stealth walking forward and backward
    a. toe to heel
    b. heel to toe
    c. roll on the side of the foot

2. Noises: use natural noises to cover movement; trains, planes, automobiles, whistles, sirens and talking.

3. Surfaces: use different surfaces
    a. start with the sidewalk or solid pavement
    b. grass/dirt: do not leave foot prints
    c. rocks, stones, gravel
    d. leaves - dry leaves can be quit challenging
    e. wet/snowy surfaces
    f. practice on surfaces in your area

4. Running Stealth

Running Stealth should be a natural part of training. It is not that the running training is necessarily for speed, rather endurance and breath control. Further, endurance training is not necessarily to get into condition for fifteen rounds of three minutes each. Rather, the warrior may have to climb or travel some distance before engaging the opponent. The warrior must be able to overcome a number of physical obstacles and still be in condition to perform physical techniques.

5. Concealment

Stealth includes not only movement, but staying still, unseen, until the proper moment to move. Many people have mastered the ability to move silently, only to find that they are unable to conceal themselves properly. The two most difficult and simplest factors in concealment are:

1. Breath control
2. Staying in one position for a longer than comfortable period of time.
> a. remain in one position for at least five minutes without moving
> b. remain in unusual positions, necessary for hiding, without moving for five to ten minutes
> c. run, or sprint a quarter of a mile, then hide with a controlled breath

II. Breath Control

Breath control is very important to all forms of martial arts. The breath provides the energy and fuel to continue moment to moment. In running there are several activities one can work on in their breath control.

a. Concentrate on the natural breathing. Pay attention to the direction of your breathing. Pay attention to the rate and volume of your breathing. Work on slowing down your breathing while running. Breathing while running should become as natural as breathing while walking or even while at rest. Practice breathing slowly and deep while running for a long distance, and or while running sprints in a short distance.

b. Stealth. Breath control and endurance is an essential element to advanced stealth techniques. The warrior may find the perfect place of concealment. However, if they are panting and coughing because of improper breathing through running to, or climbing into place, then their stealth location and techniques will quickly be compromised. Practice sneaking up on people in the street, without them knowing you are coming until you pass right next to them.

III. Intention

Use a long run for meditation. Find a course for a long run that you feel comfortable with. One relatively safe from dangerous traffic, animals and so forth. Run until you become tired and first start to think about stopping. At that time you can begin to meditate or go into a subconscious state while continuing to run.

Note: Stealth is easy to practice nearly all the time. Work on having a soft step at work, at school, at home and every place that you walk. Continually walk to, around, and by people without them noticing you until the last minute, or perhaps not at all.

HOSHIN GAMES

BUS STATION

Objective: To understanding how to blend into a crowd.

Type: Stealth

Participants: Individual

Materials: A city bus, train, or plane terminal.

Method: Have participants go into a crowded bus station and look around for fifteen seconds then come back out. Have participants go in one at a time. When everyone has had their brief turn, compare what and who was seen, and what and who was not seen. Have participants return for about thirty seconds to see what was missed. Determine the characteristics of the people and things commonly not seen the first time.

Variation: Try this at the Mall. Find an area where people are setting and quickly scan the area. Take a second look with more focus and find who and what you missed with the initial scan.

Learning Style: Reflective, Multi-sensory, Global

FIND SOKE'S NOSE

Objective: To develop the sense of observation of small details.

Type: Stealth

Participants: Group

Materials: Any small object between one or two inches square.

Method: The object will be clearly identified to all the participants. One person will be chosen to hide the object, at least partially in plain view. The other group members will indiscriminately look for the object while they are doing their regular class activities. Time looking for the object specifically should not be permitted. Whoever finds the object will identify that they have done so. They will hide the object in the room as soon as they have a chance without being seen. Repeat the process. This is generally an on-going class activity.

Learning Style: Intuitive, Inductive, Multi-sensory

GAUNTLET I

Objective: To develop stealth in a highly hostile environment.

Type: Stealth

Participants: Group

Materials: Bean bags, flour socks, rope, water balloons, etc.

Method: Participants will negotiate a given corridor of terrain using stealth. Other group members will take position along the corridor with objects of assault. The initial participant is to move through the defined corridor using stealth and natural objects as protection while under fire.

Learning Style: Intuitive, Multi-sensory, Kinesthetic

HIDE AND SEEK

Objective: To develop stealth skills.

Type: Stealth

Participants: Group

Materials: Tennis balls.

Method: Play is similar to regular hide and go seek. Here, the person who is 'it' must throw a weapon (tennis ball) to tag someone else. There is no home base. The participants should **not** know who's 'it' at the beginning of the game. This secrecy heightens the concern that each and any other participant may be the one after you. Play should be continuous. When a player finds and tags another, the one tagged is now 'it' and the other can return to hiding.

Variation: Designate one or more objectives for the hiders to move to during the activity so that they can not stay still in an extremely concealed location.

Learning Style: Intuitive, Multi-sensory, Kinesthetic.

ROCK

Objective: Control of physical movement and desire.

Type: Stealth

Participants: Individual

Materials: None.

Method: The main essence of this activity is very slow movement. Participants practice moving at an imperceptive speed. This can take the form of standing from a seated position or in moving across a given area. When observed at any moment, no movement should be perceived. However, over five or ten minutes the shape or location of the participant should change.

Learning Style: Kinesthetic, Reflective, Intuitive

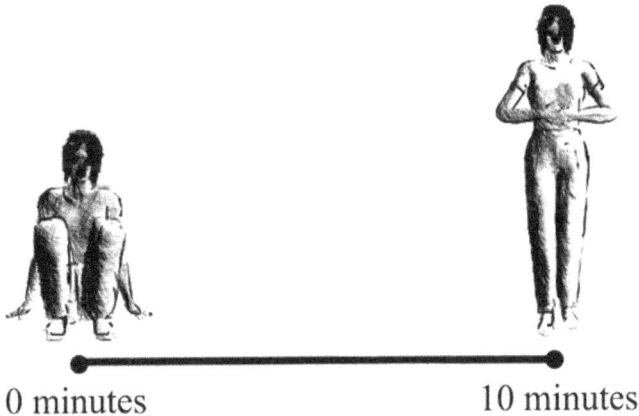

0 minutes   10 minutes

SENTRY I: CROSSING THE ROAD

Objective: To practice crossing a guarded road.

Type: Stealth

Participants: Group

Materials: The beginning practice of this activity should take place along a trail in the woods.

Method: Find a trail in the woods that is relatively flat. At a point post a couple of sentries. The sentries should keep watch of the trail for someone walking down the trail, but not to stare at it. The other participants will stealthily move to the underbrush next to the trail without being seen. The participants will then one at a time attempt to cross the road without being seen. The sentries will count the number of participants they saw crossing the trail. It is important to both stay a safe distance away from the sentries to not be seen, and at the same time challenge yourself on how close you can be to the sentries and still not be seen.

Learning style: Intuitive, Inductive, Global

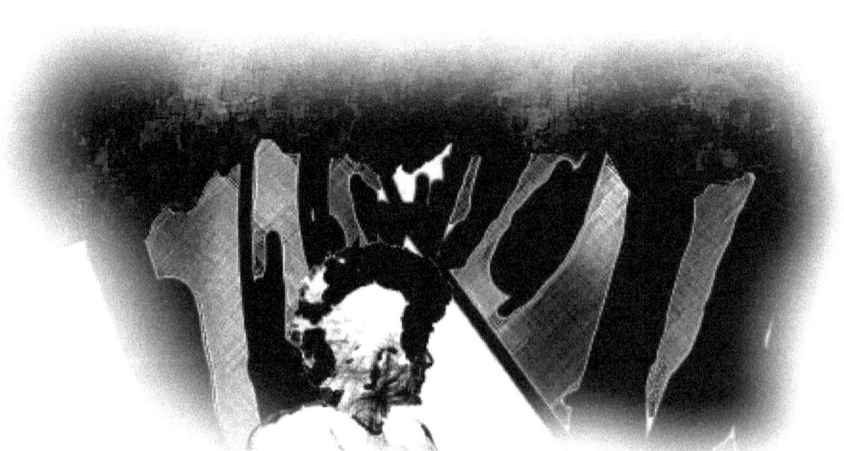

SENTRY II: PATROL EVASION

Objective: To learn to avoid those who want to do you harm.

Type: Stealth

Participants: Group

Materials (location): Wooded or urban environment.

Method: Have one group be guards. The participants are to move around a given area while at the same time avoiding the guards. Participants should challenge themselves to evade at the last second and yet remain as close as possible to the guards. Participants may be able to obtain information verbally or visually. Participants can prepare to hide 10 minutes and 100 yards from the guards, but that is not the purpose of this activity. Work on being close, concealed, and mobile.

Variation: Take these skills to a local restaurant or public assembly. Practice on gathering info while remaining hidden.

Learning Style: Intuitive, Multi-sensory, Kinesthetic

SNEAK UP I: THE DEFENSE

Objective: To develop the ability in identifying approaching danger and harm.

Type: Stealth

Participants: Partner

Materials: A quiet location or room.

Method: One person will sit at one end of the area in a semi-meditative posture, facing away from the center of the area. The second person will begin at the opposite end of the area. The second person will attempt to sneak up to the first person. The first person will sense the path the first person's approach and indicate, by pointing to the person, when that person is about three to five feet away. The first person will then turn around and look at where the second person is to verify what was sensed. It is very important that the second person focus their attention on doing harm to the first person. This focus can be a blow to the head, a strike to the back, or a choke to the throat. The other participants in the group should be quiet; not talking, however other natural noises will not hinder this activity.

Learning Style: Intuitive, Reflective, Global

SNEAK UP II: THE ATTACK

Objective: To practice sneaking up on someone without being detected.

Type: Stealth

Participants: Partner

Materials: A quiet location.

Method: This activity is structure exactly like SNEAK UP I with one exception. The second person, the person moving to attack the first person, will not focus their attention onto attacking the first person until they are within five or six feet of that person. Instead, the second person will focus on an object in the peripheral area. The two most commonly used methods are first, to focus on a spot in the current direction of motion, when the direction is change, change the spot of focus, and so forth. This will cause a number of Fuso spots and will lead to the confusion of location. The second is to always focus on location in the peripheral area, regardless of the direction of approach. For example, focus your intent on a spot thirty yards to the left of the first person while approaching from the right or the center.

Note: Many people have experienced this activity without realizing what was going on. One example is that if you were ever in a store, a parking lot, or a crowded area and you suddenly looked up at someone, you caught their energy projection and it was so strong that your natural instincts told you to check it out. Too often, however, we allow our conscious mind to dominate and try to rationalize this occurrence. Too much of the rational conscious mind will suppress the ability to detect harmful energy as it approaches in space or time.

Learning Style: Intuitive, Reflective, Global

SURVEILLANCE CAMERA

Objective: To become aware of the surroundings in an urban environment.

Type: Stealth

Participants: Group

Materials: None.

Method: Walk through several blocks and buildings of a city. Note the location of all surveillance cameras, including the direction and field of vision. Return through the same course and identify cameras missed the first time. Go through the same general course the third time, this time taking a path avoiding the cameras' view.

Learning Style: Intuitive, Inductive, Visual

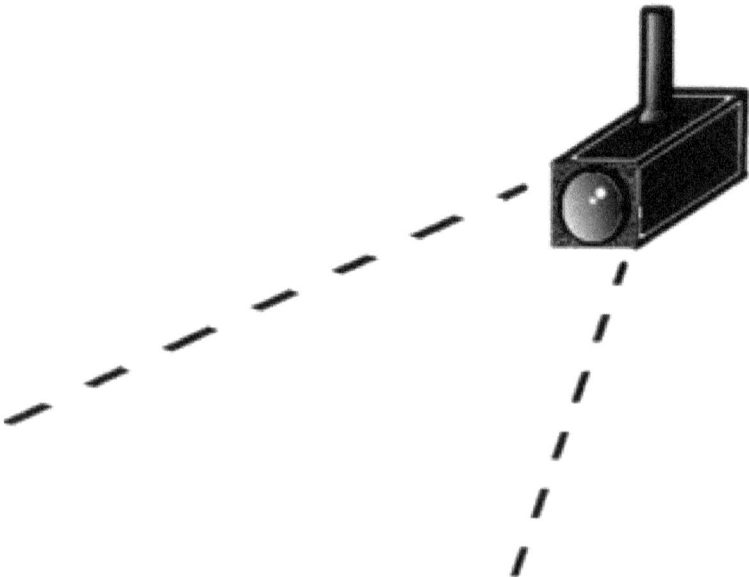

THREE MAN TEAM

Objective: To practice moving through obstacles that are more difficult in moving a group through, rather than an individual.

Type: Stealth

Participants: Group

Materials: A wooded area or a busy urban setting.

Method: This game is played similar to HIDE AND SEEK, with the exception that the participants are in multi-person groups. Being stealthy in a group or a small team presents more and different challenges than as an individual. To be most effective, the members of the team must develop the ability to intuitive understand their team members, as well as to sense the impending danger from others. This activity can become very complex from an energy perspective.

Learning Style: Intuitive, Multi-sensory, Inductive

HOSHIN GAMES

TEAM BUILDING ACTIVITIES

HOSHIN GAMES

NITRO CROSSING

Objective: To develop cooperation and management skills in a crisis.

Type: Team Building

Participants: Group

Materials: A rope tied securely to hold a person swinging. A bucket of water.

Method: All members of the group need to traverse an area of about ten feet wide using a swinging rope. There should be a defined line where participants can not cross at both the starting side and the ending side. Each member of the group must get from one side to the other without touching the ground inside the defined lines. At some point, the group must also get a bucket of water, about 3/4 filled, across the expanse without spilling any of it.

Variations:
    a. A time limit may be established.
    b. Any errors would be a cause for a restart.
    c. Transport a wounded person.

Learning Style: Intuitive, Inductive, Social

NUCLEAR MELT DOWN

Objective: To practice calm and effective leadership and cooperative skills in a crisis situation.

Type: Team Building

Participants: Group

Materials: A defined perimeter area of approximately 15 to 20 feet in diameter; two or three cans (buckets, etc.), each of a different size (each should be able to fit inside another); and several ropes and some pieces of wood.

Method: Each can is placed inside the perimeter area at least one foot from each other. The smallest can will be filled about eighty percent full with water. The objective of the activity is to get all the cans in one group (one inside the other), and then bring the whole group out at one time, without anything touching the surface of the inside perimeter area. Participants will be given a time limit to create tension and crisis. In order to succeed, participants must be calm and steady, even though they are facing disaster and their time is running out.

Learning Style: Reflective, Kinesthetic, Global

POT-OF-GOLD

Objective: To develop creative thinking during stress and frustration.

Type: Team Building

Participants: Group

Materials: A bucket (pickle barrel), at least two ropes long enough to traverse the diameter of the circle with about ten to fifteen feet extra on either side, some shorter ropes, and extra stuff that may look usable but is not necessary, may also be included.

Method: Establish a perimeter, somewhat circular, about 75 feet in diameter. Place a plastic bucket (a pickle barrel), or other similar object, near the center of the defined area. Participants are to pick the bucket up and move it from the center of the circle to outside the edge without anything touching inside the perimeter of the circle. To make this a more entertaining exercise, place the bucket between two large trees that are opposite each other, just outside the perimeter. Inevitably a group will want to send one of their own out on a rope to pick up and carry off the bucket. It has never worked for many reasons. If anything touches the ground the group must start over. Illusion and confusion is part of the exercise.

Learning Style: Intuitive, Inductive, Social, Global

SPEED TOUCH

Objective: To develop group problem solving and cohesiveness.

Type: Team Building

Participants: Group

Materials: Any small object (tennis ball, bean bag, etc.)

Method: This activity is excellent in when working with a group of people who are starting to come together as a team. Challenge the group to find out how fast they can pass the tennis ball among their members so that each member of the group can touch the ball at least once. Remember, this activity is called "Speed Touch", not "sort of fast touch".

Note: Sequentially, the best time to introduce this activity is immediately after TEAM JUGGLING.

Learning Style: Reflective, Social, Youthful

SPIDER WEB

Objective: Using physical and mental strength in overcoming an obstacle.

Type: Team Building

Participants: Group

Materials: Long piece of rope and several smaller pieces. Create a web like construction with the pieces of rope, between two trees, about five feet high, with holes about three feet in diameter.

Method: Try to have at least one space (including over the top and under the bottom) for each participant. All participants are to go through a different area in the web without touching it. Adaptations can be made depending on the size and condition of the group and the make-up of the web.

Learning Style: Kinesthetic, Inductive, Social

TEAM JUGGLING

Objective: To learn to help others in a cooperative process.

Type: Team Building

Participants: Group

Materials: Bean bags for about three-fourths of the participants.

Method: This activity is structured much the same as BEAN BAG TOSS, except now the leader will introduce more bean bags. Start with tossing three bean bags so that the group can develop a kind of rhythm. Once this pattern has been established, attempt to introduce as many being bags to the group as possible.

Variations:
   a. To be successful each person must throw to the same person each time. To cause problems for the group, the leader can vary the person they start with.
   b. Introduce different size and weights of objects
   c. Juggle with weapons, equipment, or other gear

Learning Style: Kinesthetic, Rhythmic, Social

TEAM JUMP ROPE

Objective: To develop group cohesion and confidence.

Type: Team Building

Participants: Group

Materials: A long rope (at least twenty feet in length).

Method: To experience team jump rope you need about twelve people. Two people will twirl the rope. This is generally the leader(s), or a participant that is unable to jump. Twirl relatively slow and with a big loop. Have the rope touch the ground on the bottom of the swing. Rules of team jump rope are that each person must run into the twirling loop for one jump, on one twirl, then exit the other side. The next person in line moves into the twirling rope, without having an empty twirl in between the previous jumper. Repeat the process until all participants have jumped. As an extension, try to get the group of participants to accomplish thirty consecutive jumps (or more) by having jumpers go to the end of the line after their successful jump and continue to jump.

Learning Style: Kinesthetic, Multi-sensory, Social

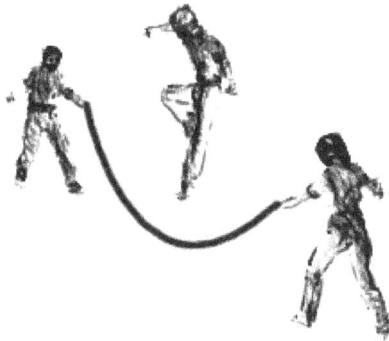

TRANSPORT

Objective: To develop team problem solving and cohesion.

Type: Team Building

Participants: Group

Materials: Four metal pipes between 2in. to 4in. in diameter
One rope 6ft. or longer
One 2 x 10, 6 to 10ft
One 2 x 4, 6 to 8ft

Method: This is a basic 'everyone on this side of the line to everyone on that side of the line' activity. Provide the group a given distance depending on their experience, from about 20' to 50'. Participants are given the above supplies, more or less, and are required to get all the members of their group from one side of the area to the other without touching the ground. If anyone falls, they start all over.

Learning Style: Social, Kinesthetic, Deductive

TROLLEY

Objective: To develop team cohesion, cooperation, and communication.

Type: Team Building

Participants: Group

Materials: Two 4' x 4', 6 to 8ft long, six to eight ropes 8' long.

Method: Trolleys can be made for a group of two to eight people. Although trolleys can be made for larger numbers, it is much more practical and educational to use multiple trolleys. A four foot trolley will carry two to three people (space each person about 2 feet apart). An eight to ten foot trolley will carry up to eight people. Each group of participants will need two trolleys with a foothold for each foot (like a sandal) and two ropes looped through the 4' x 4' to use as a handle. The team must walk on the trolley in unison to a given destination. The easiest scenario is an out and back course on a hard surface. A more advanced version includes the negotiation of obstacles or the use of only non-verbal cues.

Learning Style: Kinesthetic, Multi-sensory, Social

HOSHIN GAMES

SURVIVAL GAMES

ALTER EGO

Objective: To practice an alter identity and learn to blend in different settings.

Type: Survival

Participants: Individual

Materials: Depends on the character chosen.

Method: The participants will assume the identity of a person of a completely different social class. The character of a homeless person is often used in beginning exercises, although any character is acceptable. It is more difficult to assume the character of extremely wealthy or intellectual individuals. The participant should, dress, talk like, and practice the mannerisms of their chosen character. The activity can start with simple observation and note taking, progressing into spending up to several days in the alter ego character.

Learning Style: Reflective, Social, Multi-sensory

CAPTURE THE FLAG I

Objective: To practice and coordinate group mission skills.

Type: Survival

Participants: Group

Materials: Two different colored flags on a stick.

Method: This is the basic version that everyone has played at some time as a child. Divide into two groups of participants. Each group will establish their based camp by placing their flag in plan site. Each group is to deploy its members as to both attacking and capturing their opponent's flag while defending their own.

Note: Generally this game is played in a rural area. Try an urban version.

Learning Style: Kinesthetic, Social, Intuitive

CAPTURE THE FLAG II

Objective: To practice individual stealth techniques.

Type: Survival Skills

Participants: Group

Materials: An object. Usually a barn or other structure that can be entered.

Method: Designate a target (preferably a building) to be entered. The building will have a minimum number of guards. The main path, check points, and general area may also be guarded (minimally). Participants are to use stealth to approach and enter the target without getting caught. A time limit should be established.

Note: Guards may use tennis balls or water balloons as weapons.

Learning Style: Kinesthetic, Intuitive, Inductive

CONVERSATIONAL TAIJUTSU

Objective: To identify and defend against emotional attacks.

Type: Survival Skills

Participants: Partner

Materials: Uke (training partner)

Method: Have the uke begin a verbal attack toward you. Pay attention to the direction of the attack, the intensity of the energy, and how it hits you emotionally and mentally. Begin to move your body to a defensive posture as you are also moving your mind and emotions out of the way. Practice until you can move your mind and emotions without using your body. Practice different types of verbal responses to the different types of directed conversation. Those who know the elemental attitudes can easily counter their uke.

Note: This activity is extremely helpful in improving business and personal relationships.

Learning Style: Verbal, Social, Inductive

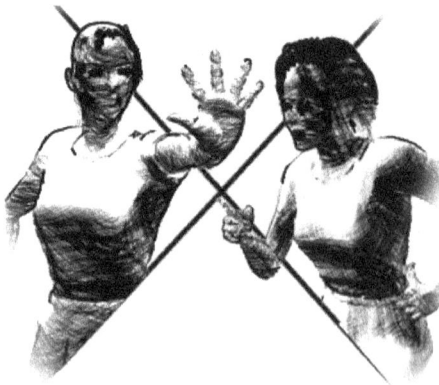

DECISION MAP

Objective: To experience the advantages and disadvantages of getting help from others in the decision making process and to improve reconnaissance skills.

Type: Survival Skills

Participants: Trio

Materials: Paper, pencil, compass, and map of the area.

Method: Divide the participants into groups of three to five students each. Select several familiar area locations/objectives. Have each team find several different routes to get to the various objectives on the map. Keep track of each of the routes that are considered. Have the teams discuss what they like and dislike about each route. Finally, have them choose one route to each destination.

Variation: Place obstacles on the easiest or most often chosen route, i.e. Sentries, Snipers, Road Blocks, etc.

Learning Style: Kinesthetic, Deductive, Multi-sensory

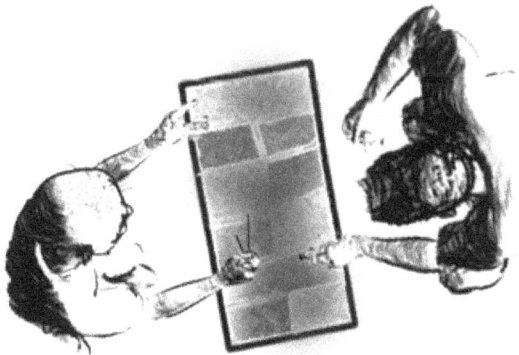

DETECTIVE

Objective: Students will use clues to understand misbehavior. Then practice 'mental taijutsu'.

Type: Survival Skills

Participants: Group

Materials: A series of short stories with various kinds of behavior.

Method: Students are to solve the mystery of behavior using the following clues.

Clue 1: Behavior can follow a pattern or cycle. Everyone wants to get along. When we do not feel as if we are getting along with others, we get discouraged. We can become confused about how to fit in and to get along.

Clue 2: All behavior has a purpose. The four main purposes or payouts of misbehavior are attention, power, revenge, or giving up.

Clue 3: You can tell what goal a person is pursuing by looking at the feelings of people around the person. These are some feelings that go with different goals: attention gives irritation and annoyance; power gives anger and frustration; revenge gives the feeling of hurt; giving up gives the feeling of hopelessness and frustration.

After the stories have been heard students identify the behavior. Asked students to consider what feelings they would have around a person like the one they just read about.

Learning Style: Verbal, Deductive, Intuitive

Detective

Espionage

ESPIONAGE

Objective: To accomplish an espionage mission without getting caught or killed.

Type: Survival Skills

Participants: Group

Materials: A piece of paper, pencil, and one tennis ball per participant. Conduct activity in a large urban setting or university campus.

Method: Give the participants an assignment, such as to get the numbers of all the pay telephones or serial number from copy machines. The objective is to get as many of the numbers as you can in a specific amount of time. At the same time, all other participants are doing the same thing. Each participant carries a weapon (tennis ball is good for public places). When a participant gets hit with a tennis ball they must give their list of numbers to the person who hit them.

Note 1: This creates a variety of options for the participants. They can stealthily move around getting numbers; they can wait till near the end of the time, ambush someone and take there names; or to create a false list of numbers, giving this list to the ambusher and retaining the true list, which may or may not be hidden somewhere else.

Note 2: When an encounter occurs, participants may throw or tag with their tennis ball. When the opponent is hit they must give their list to get their tennis ball back. The winner, however, may choose to keep the tennis ball, eventually accumulating multiple. After the encounter the participants must either work together or leave the area in separate directions.

Learning Style: Kinesthetic, Multi-sensory, Intuitive

IDENTIFICATION

Objective: Information gathering.

Type: Survival Skills

Participants: Individual

Materials: Crowded shopping area.

Method: Pick a person at random and follow them for a period of time. This exercise is done very easily in a mall where there are many people. Try to determine what size and color of clothing the person likes, the kinds of food they eat, the kind of car they drive, and so on. If you feel that you have been noticed and your quarry becomes suspicious, break off the exercise. Review what worked and what didn't before repeating the exercise. Remember, this is only an exercise to practice a skill. Do not do anything illegal!

Learning Style: Multi-sensory, Inductive, Global

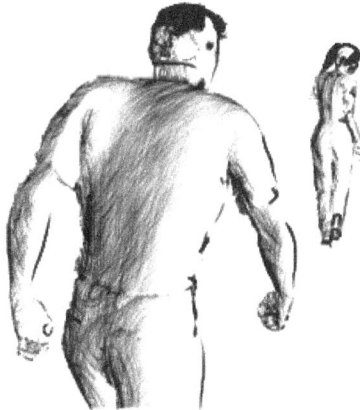

ORIENTEERING

Objective: To learn to tell direction in a strange environment.

Type: Navigational Skills

Participants: Individual

Materials: Compass, map.

Method: Orienteering is a relatively common activity. It is the method of going from point A, to point B, to point C and so on. Some variations to help Hoshin skills are to go through a course without a compass or map, using pace walking, wind direction, sun, stars, smell, and sounds as bearing points.

Variation:
  A. describe direction in degrees of angle
  B. describe distance in feet or yards
  C. describe trails in number of paces
  D. set obstacles that have to be negotiated
  E. in a classroom setting; have students move from point to point to find test questions or notes.

Learning Style: Kinesthetic, Deductive, Sequential

PACE WALKING

Objective: To develop measuring and estimating abilities in distances.

Type: Navigational Skills

Participants: Individual

Materials: A measured distance; a running track is a good place to start).

Method: Using a measuring device, measure the distances of 10 yards, 20 yards, in 50 yards in a straight line. The participants, using a natural walk, count the number of their steps for each of the distances. Use math skills to determine the length for their stride, and how many strides for 10, 20, and 50 yards they consistently take. A person about six feet tall will generally take about twelve paces per ten yards. A 6' 4" person may take about eleven paces, and a 5' 8" may take about thirteen paces. Follow-up this activity by assigning the participant to measure other distances in their daily cnvironment, such as the distance to walk home.

Variation: Practice measuring differences in walking up or down hills and steps.

Note: Pace walking should be mastered before ORIENTEER-ING activities.

Learning Style: Kinesthetic, Sequential, Deductive

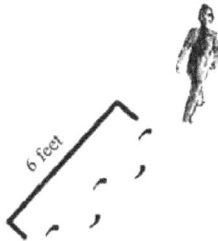

SNIPER

Objective: To identify potential lines of fire and to protect against them.

Type: Survival Skills

Participants: Group

Materials: An urban setting with many buildings. In a wooded area, use the main trail as the walk way. Tennis balls or bean bags.

Method: One person plays the role of the sniper, the other participants play the role of a person walking down a street or path. They are to find the sniper then alter their route to the next most direct path possible.

Variations:
> a. Have multiple snipers, especially with a large group of participants.
> b. Allow the participants to fire back at the sniper

Learning Style: Multi-sensory, Intuitive, Inductive

SNIPER AND BODY GUARD

Objective: To identify potential lines of fire and to protect against them.

Type: Survival Skills

Participants: Group

Materials: An urban setting with many buildings. In a wooded area, use the main trail as the walk way.

Method: This takes at least three people. One person plays the role of the sniper, the other participants are grouped in twos, one playing the victim, and one as the body guard trying to protect the victim. The body guard will walk the victim around an area (i.e. downtown, collage campus). The sniper will find a single location to attack from. The body guard is to find the sniper while protecting the intended victim. More than one sniper can be deployed if the area is large enough.

Learning Style: Multi-sensory, Intuitive, Inductive

SURVIVAL SCAVENGER HUNT

Purpose: We have all experienced a scavenger hunt at some time in the past, trying to collect odd items for points and prizes. The survival scavenger hunt has a more direct purpose. Suppose you were kidnapped, or taken hostage and held in a different city. You are able to escape your immediate area but may not be able to go directly for help. How could you survive in the urban jungle for several days while people are looking for you?

Objective: To learn how to obtain those items necessary to survive in an urban setting.

Type: Survival Skills

Participants: Individual

Materials: List of items specifically sought.

Method: Participants are to obtain and return to the group items that would increase their chance of survival in an urban area. Items may include food, mass transit token, towels, first aid supplies, alternate clothing, etc.). Give higher point values for more important items, and fewer points for less important or common items. For example a free bus token would have more value than a fast food discount coupon.

Learning Style: Multi-sensory, Intuitive, Inductive

URBAN OBSTACLE COURSE

Purpose: Generally, the best tactic is to turn and run. If you can go over walls and fences, through cracks in the wall or fences, run up and down stairs, and so on, faster and better than your pursuers, then your chance for survival and freedom are greatly increased.

Objective: To develop evasion and stealth skills in an urban environment.

Type: Survival Skills

Participants: Individual

Materials: Common city obstacles.

Method: Set a course of obstacles that a person might encounter in an urban environment. Obstacles may include going up the down escalator, taking an elevator ten floors up and the stairs down, walking through a hotel lobby without anyone looking at you, going over a wall in the parking garage, and so forth.

Learning Style: Kinesthetic, Multi-sensory, Intuitive

URBAN SURVIVAL

Objective: To practice urban survival techniques.

Type: Survival Skills

Participants: Individual

Materials: Large urban environment.

Method: Spend twenty four hours (or more) on the city streets. Participants must find a source of food, water, shelter, and restrooms.

Recommendation: It is recommended to practice this activity in pairs for safety.

Learning Style: Multi-sensory, Global, Reflective

WALL (TEAM)

Objective: To make and carryout decisions in a stressful environment.

Type: Survival Skills

Participants: Group

Materials: A flat surfaced wall and a heavy bag.

Method: The group of participants must scale a wall of at least ten feet in height using team scaling techniques. The group needs to quickly decide what the best order of movement will be to assist all of its members.

Variations:
        a. Include taking a heavy package of gear over the wall.
        b. Climb while under fire.
        c. Transport a wounded member.

Learning Style: Kinesthetic, Social, Multi-sensory

WALL DEFENSE

Objective: To practice evasive maneuvers when being chased.

Type: Survival Skills

Participants: Individual/Partner

Materials: A flat surfaced wall of approximately eight to ten feet high.

Method: The purpose of this activity is to aid in evading techniques when being confronted and chase by others. There are several variations using the wall as a rebounding tool.

Angling: Run at a wall from an angle (e.g. forty-five degrees). Time your strides so that the stride of the leg nearest the wall will be placed on the wall and the motion of the body will be reflected off at a corresponding angle.

Straight away: Run directly at a wall. Time your stride that you can place your foot on the wall and make an 180 degree turn and come straight back in the direction you approached the wall. This is an excellent strategy if being pursued closely. The force and surprise of rebounding off the wall, directly into your pursuer, is likely to startle, or even knock him off balance enough for you to get away.

Up-and over: Run straight at the wall, timing your strides so that as you approach the wall. The body will leap at the wall and literally attempt to run up the wall. Most people can get at least two strides in, generally enough to be able to grab the top of the wall and get over.

Note: Practice this activity enough to be able to judge distance and speed to the wall. This is similar to running the hurdles in track and field. Get your steps down.

Learning Style: Kinesthetic, Multi-sensory, Rhythmic

PSIONICS

Using Psionics, or psychic abilities, is generally more fun and challenging than traditional physical skills alone. The ability to make things happen and change the pattern of cause and effect can be extremely useful in everyday life, as well as in the dojo.

The psionic activities listed here start from the premise that the practitioner already has some introduction to Psi, Chi, and/or other unseen energy work. These activities are meant to refine and strengthen current levels of psychic-energy abilities. These are beginner and intermediate level activities.

Although Psionics can be practiced as its own subject, it can also be added to all of these games and any area of life. See our *Psions' Guide* for more info. Also check out Martial Arts Madness by Glenn Morris, Chapter 8, pgs. 87–106 for an additional chapter on Psionics.

HOSHIN GAMES

BEAN BAG CATCH

Objective: To practice instinctive reactions.

Type: PSI

Participants: Partner

Materials: Several small to medium size bean bags.

Method: This is a two person activity. Bean bags are used to help prevent injury. The catcher is the blind folded participant. The tosser will stand between five and ten feet from the front of the catcher. The thrower will toss the bean bag to the catcher, about chest high. The catcher will sense the throw and catch the bean bag.

Learning Style: Intuitive, Inductive, Multi-sensory

BODY EQUILIBRIUM

Objective: To practice adjusting the weight of your body to correspond with the surface which you are walking.

Type: PSI

Participants: Individual

Materials: Weak surfaces; ice, mud, snow, etc.

Method: The participant will walk across a weak surface. The participant will practice walking on these surfaces with less and less disruption to the surface. Breath control is an essential component of body equilibrium.

Learning Style: Reflective, Inductive, Global

EVASION

Objective: To develop a protective aura around the body.

Type: PSI

Participants: Trio/Group

Materials: Many bean bags and/or tennis balls

Method: This activity requires a group of three participants. Two participants will stand about 20 to 30 feet apart and toss a bean bag back and forth about chest to head level. The third participant will stand in the middle of the two participants playing catch. This person will be blind folded and stand facing one of the tossers. The tossers will throw directly to each other. It is the responsibility of the person in the middle to move out of the way and it is important that the tossers do not throw too hard or in a rhythmic pattern.

Learning Style: Intuitive, Reflective, Multi-sensory

FIRE WALK

Objective: To overcome obstacles in one's life.

Type: Goal Setting

Participants: Group

Materials: Fire pit six to ten feet long.

Method: It takes approximately three to four hours for a sufficient amount of wood to burn down to coals that are appropriate for fire walking. It is important to use some large pieces of wood. Any small sticks, under 2" in diameter will not provide a sufficient bed of coals to walk on. Use a hard rake to break up irregularities in embers. Most blisters come as a result of someone getting an ember stuck between their toes. It is recommended that an experienced fire walker be the first to walk the fire to check for any hidden problems.

All safety, first aid methods and precautions should be taken. There should be a bucket of   water for about every four or five people. Water is better than ice because the water can get to all the little cracks and crevices in your foot.

Participants may want to bring a towel to wipe their feet off before putting their shoes back on.

Participants should proceed at a slow rate, rather than lining up and running through, one after another. The bed of coals may need to be raked after every three or four people. When several people step in the same spot the coals tend to go out.

After some practice, the experienced fire walker leader can do many special things with the fire, like making it hotter or cooler, or making it feel hotter or cooler than it really is, and so on.

Recommendation: Do not try to lead your own Fire Walking activity without first training with someone who has fire walking experience. There are many subtle details that can make the difference of a safe and fun fire walking experience from one that may cause physical harm and legal action.

Learning Style: Global, Reflective, Intuitive

Note: There are many types of fire walk. Many people burn a pile of wood, rake it, and then walk across the ashes, hoping not to get burned. However, under the guidance of a leader, fire walking can bring great enlightenment. There are also several safety precautions that need to be taken.

FUMBLE

Objective: To practice causing a temporary loss of coordination in others.

Type: PSI

Participants: Individual

Materials: None

Method: The participant will sit near a pathway or walkway where a large group will be passing by. The participant uses energy to cause passers-by to trip, drop items, and so forth.

Variation: A warm-up exercise to FUMBLE is ITCH-IT. Having someone itch their face or arm is often a little easier than to cause them to fumble, although the energy is the same.

Learning Style: Intuitive, Inductive, Global

GAUNTLET II

Objective: To practice allowing your senses to keep you out of trouble.

Type: PSI

Participants: Group

Materials: Blindfolds.

Method: One of the participants will stand at one end of the floor and place a blindfold around their eyes. The other members of the group will randomly stand in one place around the room. The blind folded member will walk from one end of the room to the other without bumping into any of the sighted participants.

Variation: Have the sighted participants hold out their arms, legs, or weapons to make it more challenging for the blindfoldies.

Learning Style: Intuitive, Multi-sensory, Inductive

HEALTH DIAGNOSIS I

Objective: To practice identifying physical abnormities of others.

Type: PSI

Participants: Group

Materials: 3 x 5 cards.

Method: Have everyone in the group write some of their physical abnormities on a 3" x 5" card. When finished, place the card into an envelope, seal the envelope, and put an identifying number on it. Place all the envelopes in a pile and shuffle them. Randomly select an envelope and locate the identifying number. The group members should focus on this identifying number. Begin to draw a picture of the person associated with the identifying number. (This is a psi class, not an art class). Place a mark(s) on the picture of the body where you sense there is an injury.

Learning Style: Intuitive, Global

HEALTH DIAGNOSIS II

Objective: To practice identifying physical abnormities of others.

Type: PSI

Participants: Group

Materials: A gray wall.

Method: This activity involves the reading of auras. If you have some experience in aura reading then you are ahead of the curve. The best place to begin to read auras is if the subject were to sit in a semi-meditative posture a few feet in front of a gray wall. The other members of the group will sit about ten to fifteen feet away and gaze at the person in the semi-meditative posture. The basic energy field of a person is relatively easy to see. In time, you will be able to distinguish shades of color (and other things). Darker shades of color will indicate a problem, generally physical, lighter shades will indicate open energy flows and a healthy body.

Learning Style: Intuitive, Reflective, Inductive

LAND MINE

Objective: To develop the sense of danger and avoiding danger.

Type: PSI

Participants: Group

Materials: Objects that represent mines (bean bags, pillows, etc.).

Methodology: A specially defined area will be identified as the mine field area. Objects such as pillows or focus mitts are scattered over the area representing land mines. Participants will walk through the mine field blindfolded, using their sense of danger to avoid obstacles. Participants should experiment with trusting their feeling, especially during the first several attempts. Participants should try to become aware of their sense of overriding the feeling of danger.

Variations: If participants are having a difficult time sensing the land mine objects as dangerous, and therefore not being able to avoid them, other students may project dangerous intent onto those areas to increase the dangerous energy.

Learning Style: Intuitive, Multi-sensory, Global

LIFT (TWO FINGER LIFT)

Objective: To understand the mind's ability to change shape and mass.

Type: PSI

Participants: Group

Materials: None.

Method: Have one participant lie prone on the ground, face up, hands across their chest. Have four to six other participants placed around the person's body ready to lift that person using only two fingers, the pointer and middle fingers. The first time for the lift the individual being lifted will focus on being as light as a feather. This will allow the person to be lifted. The second time they are to be lifted they will focus on being as heavy as iron. It will be very difficult if not impossible for the lifters to get the person off the ground. Repeat with the focus back and forth.

Note: It is recommended that all participants participate either as the lifted, the lifters, or safety spotters.

Learning Style: Intuitive, Multi-sensory, Global

PSYCHIC OBSTACLE COURSE

Objective: To practice avoiding objects that possess negative energy.

Type: PSI

Participants: Group

Materials: Any items to mark a spot on the course. That is, a focus mitt can represent an object to go over or around, two focus mitts could represent a door or wall. Any item, pencils, books, tennis balls, and so forth, can be used as a marker.

Method: Each member of the group except one will establish their obstacle on the course. Obstacles are represented by relatively simple items placed on the floor. These members will create the details and difficulties of their obstacles using psychic energy. Between two pencils they can create a cement wall or swirling blades. The other member of the group will attempt to successfully negotiate the psychic obstacle course using their intuitive senses.

Learning Style: Intuitive, Inductive, Global

REPULSION

Objective: To move unwanted items or people out of your path.

Type: PSI

Participants: Individual

Materials: None. A crowded sidewalk. Amusement park midways are also an excellent place to practice.

Method: The practitioner will create an energy field extending about five to ten feet in front of their body. The participant will walk in a straight path while projecting the energy field. Others walking randomly across the path of the practitioner will feel the energy and alter their path to avoid it, allowing the practitioner to continue walking in a straight line.

Variations: As you become proficient with projecting this forward energy, begin to increase the speed of your pace. Start with walking a little faster. Try running, riding a bicycle, and/or while driving your car. The faster your speed of pace, the farther the forward energy must extend to be effective.

Learning Style: Intuitive, Reflective, Global

REVERSE TAG

Objective: To practice intuitive sensations.

Type: PSI

Participants: Group

Materials: Blindfolds.

Method: As the name implies, this game is played exactly opposite as regular tag (regular blind tag). Everyone is blind folded except the "IT" person. Also, the "IT" person is not the tagger, rather the avoider. The blind folded participants then try to find and tag the "IT" person. Once they tag the "IT" person then they also become an "IT" person. The blind folded people continue to seek and tag until all are not blindfolded. The game area should be large enough to move around in, but not too large to make it impossible for a blindfolded person to find at least one "IT".

Learning Style: Intuitive, Inductive, Global

SCRYING

Objective: To practice seeing beyond the present/conscious level.

Type: PSI

Participants: Individual

Materials: There are many methods of scrying. Scrying has to do with looking into a reflective object and seeing things. This is commonly seen as the magician looking into the crystal ball and seeing the future. There are as many different things to see as there are types of scrying. Some scrying surfaces include a fire, tea, or water in a silvery bowl. Notradamus used a special mirror. Mirrors can be very useful in seeing into other dimensions.

Method: Sit in a quiet and secluded location. Notradamus had a special room just for scrying. Sit with a relaxed posture and allow your eye lids to slowly close until there is just a small slit to see through. Stare at the scrying surface without blinking. The smaller the opening to the surface of the eye, the less maintenance (less blinking) it needs. In a few minutes you should begin to see things. As a safety precaution it is recommended that you set a specific time limit for your scrying sessions. Have an assistant check on you within a few minutes after the scheduled time of your scrying sessions.

Learning Style: Intuitive, Reflective, Global

SENSORY ISOLATION

Objective: To practice sensing beyond the present/conscious level.

Type: PSI

Participants: Individual

Materials: Water tank, salt water, an air raft in still water, or the floor.

Method: Choose one of the areas listen above in the materials section. They are listed in order of effectiveness. Even though the floor is listed last in the list it can be very effective and useful. Other stimulus should be removed as well. The room temperature needs to be set so that cold or warm will not be noticed. Noise is perhaps the biggest problem. This is why a specifically designed water isolation tank is preferred. In other locations reduce as much noise as possible, clocks, telephones, water, and so forth. Then use ear plugs to help reduce further noise. By letting your conscious mind relax and take some time off interpreting every subtle bit of information it receives, sensory isolation wills the practitioner to focus at the ESP level.

Learning Style: Intuitive, Reflective, Global

SHAPE SHIFT I: EXPANSION

Objective: To practice shape shifting to a larger size.

Type: PSI

Participants: Individual

Materials: None

Method: This activity is generally easier while in some motion. It is also generally momentary. However, if it is at the right moment it can be very effective. In a sense, this is similar to the technique animals use to expand their body in some way, like bushing their hair, when they feel threatened. Here, the practitioner expands their energy field which will give the temporary illusion of an increased size.

Learning Style: Multi-sensory, Inductive, Global

SHAPE SHIFT II: REDUCTION

Objective: To practice shape shifting to a smaller size.

Type: PSI

Participants: Individual

Materials: None

Method: This activity is generally easier while in motion, although relatively slower motion. It is also generally momentary. However, if it is at the right moment it can be very effective. In a sense, this is similar to the technique animals use to reduce their body in some way, so they can squeeze through a tight place in order to change locations, or to escape. Here, the practitioner reduces their energy field, which helps to temporarily reduce the person's size. This will help to squeeze into and through areas that might otherwise be inaccessible.

Learning Style: Intuitive, Multi-sensory, Reflective

SHARK AND MINNOWS

Objective: To develop the sense of impending danger.

Type: PSI

Participants: Group

Materials: Blindfolds for all participants.

Method: The participants playing the minnows will stealthily move from one side of an area to the other. The shark will try to catch the minnows going across. When a minnow is caught they become a shark. All participants are blind folded.

Variation: Only sharks are blindfolded.

Learning Style: Intuitive, Multi-sensory, Global

SILVERLINING

Objective: To practice intuitive insight of others.

Type: PSI

Participants: Partner

Materials: None; soft area to lie prone on.

Method: One person will lay flat on their back on a meditative posture. The second person will sit near the head of the first person in a seated meditative posture. At the beginning the first person will give the name of the person, or a name of a location that they will meditate on. This should be a person or location that is unfamiliar to the second person. The second person will also meditate on that name. After the meditation the second person will describe the details of the first person's meditation.

Learning Style: Intuitive, Reflective, Global

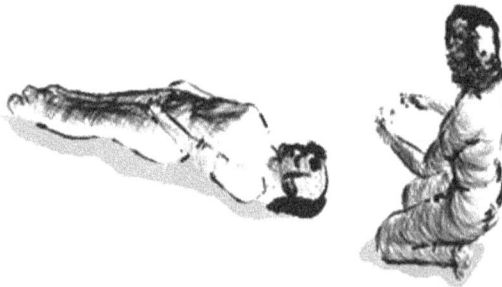

SLEEP

Objective: To practice absorbing energy from others.

Type: PSI

Participants: Individual

Materials: None

Method: The participant will sit in area where other people are also sitting. Using telekinesis, the participant will draw the energy out of another person who is not aware of the activity. Focus on the type of energy the target person has. The practitioner should notice that their target person will begin to yawn, and possibly go to sleep.

Learning Style: Intuitive, Inductive, Multi-sensory

TAKE DOWN TAG

Objective: To practice physical techniques in real situations while feeling for the extent of the attacker's energy.

Type: Physical Skill/PSI

Participants: Group

Materials: None.

Method: An advanced version of tag where there is no doubt who is 'It'. The 'It' person must perform a take-down technique as a form of tagging the other participants. The playing area should be limited in size. Time should be spent on trying to perform a take down technique, or a counter, or an escape to it while feeling for energy.

Note: Even though this is more of a physical activity, the defender should concentrate on taking the attacker's energy to its farthest point and then perform the take down, counter, or escape. Keep in mind the principles of wedging, taking space, breaking balance, reaps, redirecting energy, and so forth.

Learning Style: Kinesthetic, Intuitive, Multi-sensory

THE SEARCH FOR "IT"

Objective: To find (sense) a hidden object.

Type: PSI

Participants: Group

Materials: A small, specific object. It is easier to use an item that is composed of the same element; i.e. wood or metal.

Method: Group members should be familiar with the object, even holding it temporarily to perceive its energy. The group should not physically look when the designated person hides the object. This is best conducted in a limited space (relative to the size of the group) out doors. If this is performed indoors, in a limited area, seekers should be blind folded. Seekers then search for the "energy" of the object.

Learning Style: Intuitive, Inductive, Deductive, Social

TREE FIND I

Objective: To practice intuitive sensing in finding lost people.

Type: PSI

Participants: Group

Materials: A wooded area and blindfolds.

Method: One person will stand by a tree touching it at all times. The tree should be about thirty to forty yards into the woods. The other participants are blind folded and walk through the woods to the tree. For less experienced participants this may be down in a little grove of trees rather than in a wilderness with some under brush. Depending on the size of the area, it is recommended that a maximum of three people try to find the tree that the person is standing on at a time. Other non-active participants may be used as spotters so that the blind folded seekers do not go too far, or into a dangerous area outside the activity zone.

Variation: Depending on the size and experience of the group, more than one person may be assigned to stand on a tree giving the seekers multiple targets.

Learning Style: Intuitive, Multi-sensory, Reflective

TREE FIND II

Objective: To practice intuitive sensing in finding lost people.

Type: PSI

Participants: Group

Materials: Wooded area and blindfolds.

Method: This is similar to the TREE FIND II activity. The extension here is that the person standing next to the tree will now use their energy to push or pull the seekers off their track. This person will move the seekers to other trees, or cause them to miss the hider's tree, even if by inches.

Learning Style: Intuitive, Multi-sensory, Inductive

THOUGHT SHIELD

Objective: Thought shield is a device to limit or prevent others from entering your mind and reading your thoughts.

Type: PSI

Participants: Individual/Partner

Materials: None.

Method: Sit in a relaxed and comfortable meditative posture. During the meditation, construct a device that will greatly limit or prevent others from entering your inner thoughts. Remember that air penetration can go over or around objects and can find the tiniest cracks. Water penetration can erode stone and rust metals. Fire penetration can burn/destroy most objects.

Note: Try sitting across another person and put up a shield of any shape, size, or make-up. Have the person sitting across close their eyes and see if they can pick up your shield either through their mind or by the phosphenes behind their eyes… you'll be surprised by the amount of times you can accurately guess another's thought shield.

Learning Style: Intuitive, Reflective, Global

WHEEL WALK

Objective: To practice stealth and energy walking.

Type: PSI

Participants: Group

Materials: Blindfolds.

Method: Participants will stand around the edge of a defined area (e.g. around the wall of a room) facing into the middle. Then the participants will look to a spot on the wall anywhere across the room. Placing a blindfold over their eyes, each person, at the same time, will attempt to walk across the room to their spot on the wall.

Learning Style: Intuitive, Multi-sensory, Reflective

OBJECT FIND

Objective: To practice psi perception for finding lost items.

Type: PSI

Participants: Individual

Materials: A specific object with your energy.

Method: Even though this is listed as an individual activity, most of the practice activities may briefly involve a second person. This activity is similar to the childhood game 'hot or cold', without the verbal cues. The individual participant will have a personal object that they have put some of their own energy into. Another person will hide the object. The individual participant will then seek for and find their object.

Note: This is an excellent activity to help you find your missing car keys, or the winning lottery ticket that fell out of your pocket.

Learning Style: Intuitive, Multi-sensory, Global

PERIMETER

Objective: To practice being aware of something 'out of place'.

Type: PSI

Participants: Individual

Materials: None.

Method: This activity requires the participant to assume a meditative posture. From this meditative posture they should focus on perceptually moving from your current location, to the door, and go around the inside and/or outside of your home. Look for unlocked doors or windows, running water, or other possible problems. When something is perceived then physically check it out after the meditative perception activity.

Learning Style: Intuitive, Multi-sensory, Global

PROBLEM SOLVING

HOSHIN GAMES

ASSASSIN

Objective: To develop skills in subtle characteristics of cause and effect in large groups.

Type: Problem Solving

Participants: Group

Materials: One chair for each participant and a staging area or extra room.

Method: Everyone is seated in a circle. One person is chosen as the 'Detective' and leaves the room. One of the people in the circle is selected as the 'Assassin' and the Detective returns to stand in the middle of the circle. The Assassin kills the other members of the group one at a time by blinking their eye while looking at the victim and the Detective tries to determine who the murderer is. The Assassin's goal is to finish off every one in the circle, in the presence of the Detective, without getting caught.

Variation: Limit the Detective to only 1, 2, or 3 guesses of who's the Assassin.

Learning Style: Intuitive, Deductive, Multi-sensory

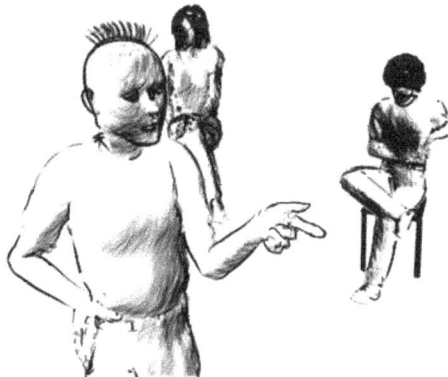

CHINA GATE

Objective: To understand different learning styles, the difficulty of making the right choice, and teamwork.

Type: Problem Solving

Participants: Group

Materials: Place markers (about the size of napkins).

Method: Place nine markers on the ground, in a row, evenly spaced, and about a foot or two apart. Have four group members stand on each marker on one side of the center marker and four group members on each marker on the other side of the center marker, leaving the center marker blank. Each the members of one side must go to the other side.

RULES:
1. Must start by facing the center.
2. You can not face the opposite direction than you started from.
3. You can only step forward, never backwards.
4. You can only step into a blank space. Spaces are indicated by the place markers set on the floor. The space in-between the markers is purely social space, and not part of the game space.
5. You can only pass one person at a time facing the opposite direction that you are facing.
6. You can never pass anyone facing the same direction that you are.
7. This is a one dimensional problem.

Variations: Eight participants is an optimal number for this group. The average problem solving time for a group this size is about 30 to 40 minutes. A group size of six or seven is likely to finish earlier, and nine or ten a little longer. For larger number of participants, divide into several groups of about seven to nine participants.

Learning Style: Intuitive, Inductive, Social

I'M GOING ON A MISSION

Objective: To develop analytic, deductive listening and verbal decoding skills.

Type: Disappearing and Finding

Participants: Group

Materials: Participants are generally seated.

Methodology: The first person, or a starter person, will establish the criteria for taking something on a mission. They would begin by saying "I am going on a mission, and with me I am going to take..." At this point they will describe something that has a particular code for taking things. For example, they may take 'green milk'. The code could be things that are green, things that have double "E's", things that come from an animal, or things that do not really exist. Each of the succeeding participants will say "I am going on a mission, and with me I am going to take..." At this point the other participants will state and object. The first person will say whether the item is allowed or denied based on their criteria. As each person states the object they may take, they are to determine by all the clues what the code is.

Learning Style: Verbal, Deductive, Social

LOOP ESCAPE

Objective: To look at all parts of a problem and learning to stop doing things that don't work in our lives.

Type: Problem Solving

Participants: Partner

Materials: A piece of rope about four feet long for each participant.

Method: Participants will work with a partner. Tie a slip knot on each end of the rope. One person puts the rope on both wrists like hand-cuffs. The other person puts the slip knot loop on one wrist, loops the rope behind and around their partner's rope and slips the end on their other wrist. At this time the partners should be standing with a somewhat figure eight joining loop. The goal of this activity to is to separate from your partner without any of the loops ever coming off your wrist.

Learning Style: Intuitive, Multi-sensory, Social

MAT BALL

Objective: To expand and go beyond rules, limits, and confinement learned earlier in life.

Type: Problem Solving

Participants: Group

Materials: One kick ball, three large bases, one cone/pillion.

Method: Establish a playing field similar to regular kickball or baseball. The exception is that first, second, and third base should be larger than normal, often the size of a mat. Home base should be a small object, often a pillion or cone. Play is similar to regular kickball with the following exceptions: only one pitch per batter. Batter must make contact or he/she is out. There is no out-of-bounds, play is 360 degrees. Any number of batters can be on first, second, or third base at the same time. Runners on third must round home and go to first to be safe. There is no safe area at home base. A run scores each time a batter rounds home and reaches first base again safely. Runners continue to run bases until there are three outs.

Learning Style: Kinesthetic, Multi-sensory, Social

MAT CROSSING

Objective: To develop cooperation in the problem solving process.

Type: Problem Solving

Participants: Group

Materials: Three, one foot square mats.

Method: A group of people must traverse an area (river, road) using only three mats to stand on. Only one participant can stand on a mat at a time. If one person touches the ground even slightly, then the whole group has to start over. Set a time limit for more advanced practitioners.

Variation: Try using small or strange objects such as cones, hand-targets, clothing, etc. Each item gives its own surprising amount of problems.

Learning Style: Intuitive, Deductive, Social

PVC RAFT

Objective: To develop cooperative and strategy during a crisis.

Type: Problem Solving

Participants: Group

Materials: Lots of PVC pipe 2" diameter or larger with end caps.

Method: Participants are to build a raft from PVC parts. They are to raft across a pond or half way down a river course. When they have reached this point they are to take the raft out of the water, take it apart, and reassemble it in a different shape, and continue on their journey. The amount of PVC pipe needed will be determined by the number of people per raft. Two or more teams may compete against time.

Learning Style: Kinesthetic, Deductive, Social

RAGING RIVER

Objective: To develop cooperation and decision making skills under stress.

Type: Problem Solving

Participants: Group

Materials: An area at least twenty feet wide designated as the river, two or three 4' x 4's, four to six feet long depending on group size, several smaller 4' x 4' pieces about one foot long randomly placed in the river representing rocks (not too close, nor too far).

Method: Participants are to get all of there group across the river at the same time without anything falling into the river.

Learning Style: Kinesthetic, Deductive, Social

WILD WOOZY

Objective: To develop self-confidence/trust, and partner confidence/trust.

Type: Problem Solving

Participants: Partner

Materials: V-shaped rope or wire.

Method: Partners stand facing each other, putting their hands together. They are to slide their feet in the same direction. The farther they move horizontally the farther apart their feet become. This is often a part of a high ropes course performed on pre-established wires twenty feet in the air.

Learning Style: Kinesthetic, Multi-sensory, Social

PHYSICAL TECHNIQUES

HOSHIN GAMES

AERIAL ASSAULT

Objective: To develop awareness and technique under fire.

Type: Physical Skills

Participants: Trio

Materials: Bean bags, tennis balls.

Method: Participant stands in the center of three or more other participants who form a circle about twenty to thirty feet in radius. Those on the outside are armed with throwing weapons (i.e. bean bags). They will randomly throw their weapons, trying to strike the participant in the middle. The person in the middle will use techniques to avoid or capture the weapon.

Variation: After the participants have tried this a few times, tell them to concentrate on their breathing and see what techniques come into play. The four main breathing techniques are slow inhale/slow exhale, slow inhale/fast exhale, fast inhale/slow exhale, and fast inhale/slow exhale.

Learning Style: Kinesthetic, Intuitive, Multi-sensory

BIATHLON

Objective: Develop Hoshin training skills in combination.

Type: Physical Skills

Participants: Individual

Materials: Target, shuriken/darts/blow gun.

Method: Conducted similar to the winter Olympic Biathlon. Participants will run a short distance then stop to fire five rounds at a target, continue to run, fire, etc.

Learning Style: Kinesthetic, Multi-sensory, Intuitive

CANDLE MENAGERIE

Objective: To practice speed and precision in punching and kicking techniques.

Type: Physical Skills

Participants: Individual

Materials: Several candles, matches.

Method: This is similar to the CANDLE STRIKE activity, the extension here is that there are multiple targets (burning candles). The practitioner will place burning candles at various heights and angles. Each candle should be extinguished with one strike.

Note: It is recommended to master the Candle Strike activity before attempting this activity.

Learning Style: Kinesthetic, Multi-sensory, Reflective

CANDLE STRIKE

Objective: To improve speed and focus in punches and kicks.

Type: Physical Skills

Participants: Individual

Materials: One or more candles.

Method: Place a lit candle on a table. Stack the candle up to a height of normal punching. Punch at the candle stopping just in front of and not touching the candle. Strike with enough force to extinguish the flame.

Variations: Kicking, multiple candles.

Learning Style: Kinesthetic, Reflective, Intuitive

ENERGY THROW

Objective: To help visualize the throwing of energy from your body.

Type: Physical Skills/PSI

Participants: Partner

Materials: Two bean bags or two tennis balls.

Method: Partners should face each other approximately 1 foot apart. One student should be in a forward stance the other in a back stance. The student in the back stance will hold the object (bean bag) in the back hand, step forward and throw it to the second student. The second student will receive the thrown item with their forward hand and transition to a back stance at the same time. At this time each student should have reversed their original stance. The second student will step forward and throw the object to the first student who will step back and follow the energy of the ball/bean bag. Repeat.

Once student are able to coordinate the throwing and catching of one ball, they should learn to each throw and catch at the same time. Note: using two balls at one time, one object will be thrown while stepping back while it is caught stepping forward.

Learning Style: Kinesthetic, Intuitive, Social, Global

ESCAPE: HOJO JUTSU

Objective: To practice escaping from a locked handcuff.

Type: Physical Skills

Participants: Individual

Materials: One standard muffler clamp.

Method: To escape from a handcuff type situation. This is an excellent and inexpensive activity to begin to practice escaping from locked handcuffs. A standard muffler clamp is 'U' shaped that screws into a bar that crosses the open portion of the 'U' shape. The nuts on the U-bolts can be adjusted to their tightness or looseness. This will allow the practitioner to continually tighten the clamp and challenge their abilities.

Learning Style: Kinesthetic, Multi-sensory, Reflective

FLAG TAG

Objective: To practice Hoshin techniques under pressure.

Type: Physical Skills

Participants: Group

Materials: One or two flags (pieces of cloth) per participant.

Method: Each participant will place their flag at waist level with at least part of the flag exposed. The 'it' person (or persons) attempt to grab the flag of others. Participants should use Hoshin techniques to defend rather than running too much.

Learning Style: Kinesthetic, Intuitive, Multi-sensory

JIGSAW

Objective: Teaching details to a large group.

Type: Organizing Conversational Skills

Participants: Group

Materials: A series of techniques or concepts.

Method: The material to be mastered is divided equally among the group members (these could be techniques assigned to each person by the group leader, or each participants own unique movement). After each member masters their portion individually, the group comes together. Each individual is responsible for presenting his or her own material to the rest of the group and teaching how it is performed. Participants should attempt to master one another's material.

Note: This is great to use in the classroom or dojo because each person gets to show a piece of material which they have personally mastered. Everyone else gets to taste a different style, idea, concept, or area of life.

Learning Style: Social, Multi-sensory, Deductive

KNIFE CATCH

Objective: To practice rhythmic motions with weapons.

Type: Physical Skills

Participants: Partner

Materials: A knife or substitute practice item. If a practice item is substituted it should have the weighted balance of a knife and an identified sharp surface.

Method: Participants should first move the knife around in their hand to get the feel of the weight and balance. After a good sense of weight and balance is gathered, the participants stand about five to ten feet across from each other and gently toss the knife back and forth, trying to catch without getting cut or stabbed. As the participants begin to feel comfortable and confident, the pair can begin to move further apart. It is recommended to begin with non-bladed, or dull bladed weapons.

Learning Style: Rhythmic, Kinesthetic, Intuitive, Visual

LEAF STRIKE

Objective: To practice form and technique against a moving object.

Purpose: There are times when we would like to practice striking techniques, especially with weapons, but don't have sufficient targets. The autumn of the year, when the leaves of the trees are falling, or in a winter snow storm, provide excellent opportunities to practice weapon strikes with moving targets.

Type: Physical Skills

Participants: Individual

Materials: Windy fall day; weapons (bo, hanbo, sword).

Method: In the fall of the year, hold class in a wooded area when the leaves begin to fall. Use the falling leaves as targets. This will provide excellent practice for full speed striking techniques at various angels with the bo, hanbo, sword, and other weapons.

Learning Style: Kinesthetic, Intuitive, Reflective

OBSTACLE COURSE

Objective: To practice physical skills.

Type: Physical Skills

Participants: Individual

Materials: Heavy gear and an obstacle course. This can be a standard obstacle or an Urban Obstacle course. A Psychic Obstacle Course would probably not be appropriate here.

Method: The simplest structure is to have the participants carry their weapons and/or supplies with them over and through the obstacles. A more interesting version of "Obstacle Course" is to set obstacles that require the participants to use their weapons to overcome the obstacles.

Learning Style: Kinesthetic, Inductive, Intuitive

RAPID FIRE

Objective: To practice quickly feeling the energy of the attack.

Type: Physical Skills

Participants: Group

Materials: A small defined area about twelve square feet in size.

Method: One person is diagnosed as the defender (tori). The other participants (ukes) will form a single file line facing the tori. The ukes will run at the tori at about five second intervals. The tori will perform a defensive technique on a uke, and then the next, and the next, and so on. The defender must always have one foot in the defined area. This presents the defender from always backing up, and from straying into an unsafe area of practice.

Variation: Have the tori put their back to the wall, or put them in a corner. The leader can also put objects around the tori, i.e. punching bags, cones, chairs, etc. This limits their range of motion and adds another dimension to their defense. The tori should not hide behind the objects, but use them strategically.

Learning Style: Kinesthetic, Intuitive, Inductive

RECON CONTROLLER

Objective: Distinguishing and listening to a specific voice in a mass of loud voices.

Type: Organized Listening Skills

Participants: Group

Materials: One blindfold per team.

Method: Split the participants into pairs and have each pair pick a wall. One person is the 'Recon Controller', while the other is the 'Recon' person, who is blindfolded. The Recon is blindfolded because there is zero visibility, plus the wireless communication system has malfunctioned. The Recon can hear information but can not ask questions. The Recon starts at one end of the room and heads toward the other end where the Recon Controller is located. The Recon Controller tries to guide the Recon across the room through a series of obstacles. If the Recon hits an obstacle or another Recon (have several come from different directions) they must return to their base and restart.

Learning Style: Verbal, Intuitive, Multi-sensory

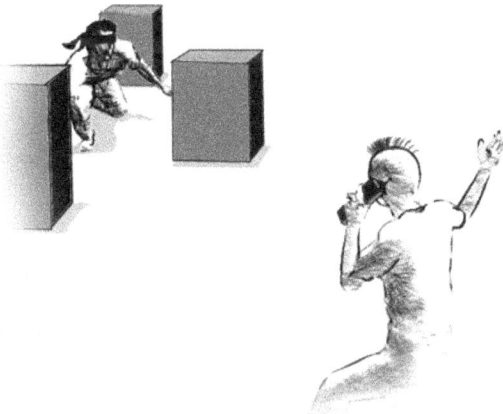

SPARRING

Objective: To simulate strong body dynamics in open hand combat.

Type: Physical Skills

Participants: Partner

Materials: Two or more small pieces of cloth.

Method: Each opponent will tuck in a piece of cloth near a body target area, such as the neck or belt area. The cloth may be placed at a specific location on the body when practicing a specific type of technique. The aggressor must pull the cloth from their opponent's place. This will cause a more realistic attack, both in speed and intensity. Multiple pieces of cloth may be used to cause the need to protect more of the body.

Learning Style: Kinesthetic, Intuitive, Global

SPARRING (DISTRACTING)

Objective: To focus on peripheral objects that may enter a confrontation.

Type: Physical Skills

Participants: Group

Materials: Mats, bean bags, and a uke (receiver of technique).

Method: The tori (performer of technique) and uke would begin to spare as normal. One or more other participants are off the mat and will periodically through a bean bag at one or all of those who are sparring.

Learning Style: Kinesthetic, Multi-sensory, Intuitive

SPRINT: 50 mt/100mt sword/hanbos

Objective: To practice weapon striking accuracy while moving.

Type: Physical Skills

Participants: Individual

Materials: Multiple striking poles. Striking poles can be of any size or shape. A common style is a braced 4" x 4" with holes drill completely through at various angles representing striking angles. The key component is to have specific striking targets and angles.

Method: This is a version of the 50 meter or 100 meter dash, with a few martial arts adjustments. At about every 5 meters to 10 meters each participant will have a striking pole in their lane. On the start, participants will run to the first striking pole and strike in with a sword (or any other weapon) in a specific location at a specific angle. The participant will continue onto their next striking pole, performing another strike at a specific location at a specific angle. This will continue until the end of the course.

Note: If in a group, you can have the extra members stand at every 5 or 10 meter spot either holding a target out for the runner to strike, or become targets themselves. This also challenges the person to control their weapon.

Learning Style: Kinesthetic, Deductive, Multi-sensory

TANK

Objective: To give, listen to, and follow directions in a stressful situation.

Type: Organized Listening

Participants: Group

Materials: One blindfold per group. Small, soft pieces of ammunition (rolled up pieces of paper). Here, pieces of paper are preferred for ammunition rather than tennis balls because the tennis balls may roll too far after being thrown. If the activity were conducted in a relatively confined area, tennis balls could be used.

Method: Pair participants in groups of two. One person becomes the tank while the other becomes the tank commander. The person in the role of the tank is blindfolded. The tank commander will give verbal instructions to the tank and is not allowed to physically interact. Begin with a practice trial. Scatter the ammunition on the floor, then have the tank commander guide the tank person to find, pick-up, and fire at a target. After the trial run teams can compete against other teams by trying to hit the other team's tank with the ammunition. Trade roles and play again.

Learning Style: Verbal, Kinesthetic, Multi-sensory

WEAPON CATCH

Objective: To improve visual/spatial relationships and coordination.

Type: Physical Skill

Participants: Partner

Materials: Weapons (screwdriver, tonto, sai).

Method: Similar to KNIFE CATCH, but a little more dangerous. With a partner, play catch with the weapon, always catching the weapon by the handle. Begin by throwing the weapon flat, then with a slight rotation. Begin practicing with screwdrivers. They are generally not as dangerous, nor illegal.

Learning Style: Kinesthetic, Multi-sensory, Reflective, Visual

WEAPON SPEED STRIKE

Objective: To develop foot work and technique in multiple striking attacks.

Type: Physical Skill

Participants: Individual

Materials: Four to eight 2' x 4' six feet long and a stand to support the wood vertically.

Method: Drill three 2in holes in the 2 x 4's at a low, middle, and high striking level. Make a stand for the 2 x 4's so that they will set vertical to the ground. Place the vertical poles eight to ten feet apart in four or eight directions. Use medium range striking weapons such as bo, hanbo, or sword to strike though the holes at various levels and directions.

Learning Style: Kinesthetic, Reflective

HOSHIN GAMES

There are many more variations of *Hoshin Games* with a common premise. The better the individual, or team, is likely to perform, the more restrictions that might be imposed on them. Restrictions can include, but are not limited to not being able to talk, not being able to see, being partially handicapped (not being able to use one arm or leg), time limits, material limits or loads, and/or while under fire.

The leader can also emphasize a particular elemental attitude to each game. After the group has mastered or practiced a particular game enough times, encourage them to concentrate of their breathing. Tell them to either breathe with a...

1. slow inhale, slow exhale
2. slow inhale, fast exhale
3. fast inhale, fast exhale
4. fast inhale, slow exhale

Correspond these to their correct attitudes and movements and see what it adds to the game. Check out Dr. Glenn Morris's *Pathnotes of an American Ninja Master, Shadow Strategies, Martial Arts Madness,* and *Quantum Crawfish Bisque for the Clueless Soul,* and Dr. Porter's *Mandala Therapy* and *The Psions' Guide* or ask on our Yahoo Public Discussion Group found at www.hoshin.us for more info on this subject.

The variations are infinite. Have fun, be safe, and use your imagination. Take advantage of the Skills Checklist on the next page and challenge yourself to always go further.

HOSHIN GAMES

SKILLS CHECKLIST

☐ Hold, hang, and dangle from a bar for at least three minutes w/ controlled breathing. p. 3

☐ Move from a sitting to standing to sitting position etc. w/ a partner or against a wall/tree. p. 4

☐ Be able to relax and go with uncontrolled situations such as falling, be pushed, etc. p. 7

☐ Pick out and find a personal item from a pile of similar objects more than 50% of the time. p. 8

☐ Develop the ability to determine if and when an action needs to be taken. p. 11, 12

☐ Stand on one leg while performing average day-to-day activities without falling. p. 15

☐ Be able to do at least 10 of every type of push-up. p. 20

☐ Perform basic movements and actions while blindfolded i.e. walking, rolling, punching etc. without fumbling. p. 23, 24

☐ Scale a tree or building to the top. p. 29

☐ Move from roof top to roof top with efficiency, stealth and grace. p. 30

☐ Walk skillfully and quietly across a moving beam. p. 31

☐ Climb up a slide or ladder using specifics climbing angles. p. 32

☐ Escape through a fence or opening from a jog or run. Know what you can and cannot squeeze through quickly. p. 33, 67

☐ Escape up and down different sets of stairs quickly, safely, and quietly. p. 34

☐ Move from swing to swing (or rope to rope) quickly and efficiently. p. 35

☐ Master basic stealth walks going forward and backward. p. 45

☐ Naturally blend your walking with external noises. p. 45

☐ Eliminate leaving footprints when walking. p. 45

☐ Be able to run with controlled breathing, while in stealth, and able to fully defend yourself afterwards. p. 46

☐ Stay in an uncomfortable position for 5-10 min. p. 46

☐ Easily enter a meditative/subconscious state while running/exercising for an extended period of time. p. 46

☐ Determine who the attacker is in an unknown situation. p. 52

☐ Be able to change to a different body position without

any visible movement.   p. 53

☐   Make your way past, or close, towards a number of sentry guards.   p. 54

☐   Collect information from a group of people while remaining concealed and mobile.   p. 55

☐   Detect harmful energy through your sixth sense.   p. 56

☐   Mask your intent as you sneak up on someone.   p. 57

☐   Consciously avoid and walk around surveillance cameras throughout the day/night without being obvious   p. 58

☐   Stay hidden as a whole group when moving through urban, forest, and open terrain.   p. 59

☐   Carry a cumbersome object with you as you swing across a rope.   p. 63

☐   Pass through an obstacle that is in motion.   p. 69

☐   Assume the role of another personality type and stay in that character for 1-3 days.   p. 75

☐   Successfully defend against verbal attacks.   p. 78

☐   Trail an unsuspecting stranger for an extended period of time while taking the appropriate action if spotted.   p. 83

☐   Gain a basic knowledge of orienteering.   p. 84

☐ Accurately and instantly measure your distance without the use of physical tools. p. 85

☐ Use all of your knowledge up to this point to sniper someone from afar (in a game type setting only!).
p. 86

☐ Use your skills to practice being a bodyguard for your team mates and friends in the correct circumstances.
p. 87

☐ Search for items that you would use if you were stranded in a city or town. p. 88, 90

☐ Find a set of physical obstacles in an urban type setting and over come them. p. 89

☐ Master the different ways to recherché off of a wall and attack your pursuer. p. 92

☐ Build a protective aura around your body. p. 97, 99, 100, 103, 106, 108, 115, 122, & 123

☐ Control your weight using the power of your mind.
p. 98, 107

☐ Use your intent in a more aggressive form. p. 102, 106, 108, 109, 117

☐ Use your clairvoyant abilities to sense injury & info.
p. 104, 105, 111, 112, 116, 124, 125

☐ Escape from a hand cuff or knot tied around your wrists or ankles. p. 133, 146

☐   Dodge projectiles coming from multiple angles.

p. 141, 155

☐   Become proficient in striking targets while running.

p. 142, 150, 156

☐   Distinguish a candle flame with one strike. After that, move on to multiple candle flames set at different heights.

p. 143, 144

☐   Successfully catch weapons which are thrown.

p. 149, 158

HOSHIN GAMES

INDEX

PARTICIPENTS

LEARNING STYLE

Intuitive

Sequential

Social

www.ingramcontent.com/pod-product-compliance
Lightning Source LLC
Chambersburg PA
CBHW031257090426
42742CB00007B/494